CAKESPY

PRESENTS

Sweet Treats for a Sugar-Filled Life

JESSIE OLESON

SASQUATCH BOOKS
SEATTLE

Printed in China
Published by Sasquatch Books
Distributed by PGW/Perseus
17 16 15 14 13 12 11   9 8 7 6 5 4 3 2 1

The Elvis Whoopie Pie recipe (page 31), was created for Peanut Butter & Co. Copyright © 2010, Columbus Brands, LLC, all rights reserved. "The Bees Knee's" and "Peanut Butter & Co." are registered trademarks of Columbus Brands, LLC, used under license.

Cover and interior illustrations: Jessie Oleson
Cover and interior design and composition: Anna Goldstein
Chapter opening photographs (pages xii, 20, 44, 70, 88, 104, 116): Rachelle Longé
Cover and interior photographs: Clare Barboza

Library of Congress Cataloging-in-Publication Data is available.

ISBN-10: 1-57061-756-2
ISBN-13: 978-1-57061-756-0

Sasquatch Books
119 South Main Street, Suite 400
Seattle, WA 98104
(206) 467-4300
www.sasquatchbooks.com
custserv@sasquatchbooks.com

Contents

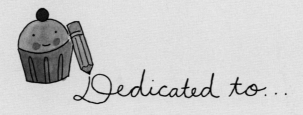

Dedicated to . . .

This totally sweet book is dedicated to SpyMom,
who taught me how to bake, eat, and draw cakes . . .
and to Mr. CakeSpy, who makes my life
sweeter each and every day.

Acknowledgments

You know how the acknowledgment page always says something like "there are too many people to possibly thank," and now I know that authors are not just saying that. But here are just a few of the too-many-to-all-be-named.

First off, a whipped-cream-and-cherry-topped thank-you to the entire staff at Sasquatch Books, who not only believed in my concept but didn't cringe when I said, "Needs more unicorns" (which I said often).

Thank you to my totally sweet agent, Gail Fortune, who not only believed in this project but helped make it happen.

A chocolate-coated thanks goes to Autumn Martin and Clare Barboza, who styled and photographed my desserts so beautifully for the interior photographs; Rachelle Longé, who handled the chapter opener photos; and Lisa Gordanier, whose assistance with recipe formatting and editing were beyond compare.

A buttercream wave of gratitude goes to my recipe testers, who included Jenny Richards, Reina Beach, and Julie DiCesare.

A cinnamon-and-sugar dusting of appreciation goes to those who inspired recipes that are found in this book: Megan Seling, Chris Jarchow, Sarah Bir, Karen Merzenich, Dani Cone, Audrey McManus, and Peabody Rudd.

Fond(ant) thoughts go to my earliest supporters: Mrs. Hillman (my 4th grade teacher), who was certain even then that I was going to be a writer and illustrator, and *Stone Soup* magazine for publishing my art at age twelve.

For keeping me engaged and excited about food, and for letting me reprint the recipes I created for them, I'd like to thank the entire staff at Serious Eats, the best food website in the world, and Peanut Butter & Co., which makes the best peanut butter in the world.

Merci encore to those who always motivate me to "just donut": Philip Longo, Rebekah Denn, C-Brod, Lily Kerson, Jennifer Pooley, James Papadopoulos, Bakerella, Becca Todd, and so, so many more.

And, of course, my family, for not cringing too much when they hear the dangerous phrase "I've got an idea . . . "

Finally, and most importantly, a thank-you à la mode with a pound of hot fudge sauce to all of the readers of my website and customers of my store. Thank you so much for surfing on over to my sweet corner of the web and enabling me to live the sweetest life possible.

Introduction

Oh, *hello*, friend. I suspect that you have excellent taste, since you've picked up my book, but I realize that you may be wondering about a few things. Please allow me to shed some light on the important subjects that are probably puzzling your pretty little head.

WHO AM I? My name is CakeSpy, and I am the Head Spy (at least that's what my business cards say) at a dessert detective agency of the same name in Seattle. My mission? Seeking sweetness in everyday life. I do this by seeking out the best recipes for baked goods and by creating sweet art-work. My findings are reported on my most excellent website, CakeSpy .com. Oh, and I also run a retail gallery in Seattle where I sell my artwork alongside that of other local artists. I even share the baked goods featured on my site with my customers—as freebies. I know what you're thinking: best job ever. *And you're right.*

HOW DID I BECOME SO OBSESSED WITH SWEETS? I could tell you the long version . . . or I could tell you two very telling anecdotes from my childhood.

FACT! After "mama" and "papa," my first word as a baby was "chocolate." According to my mother, this happened shortly after my grandmother gave me a big ol' spoonful of chocolate frosting, and apparently I knew a good thing when I tasted it. Totally true story—just ask my mom.

FACT! Around the time I was three, I developed a sweet ritual. I would steal a stick of butter from the fridge, and I would dip it into the canis-ter of sugar that resided on our counter. I would then take this forbidden treat, along with a stack of picture books, and hide under the dining room

table, looking at pictures while gnawing on my sweet plunder. Though I now prefer my books with some words and my butter and sugar with some flour and eggs, you can see how these habits developed into the seedlings of my future sweet self.

IS THIS BOOK FOR REAL? As you leaf through this book and feast your eyes on sweet recipes such as Behemoth Crumb Cake (triple the crumb, half the cake) or Glazed Cinnamon Rolls Stuffed with Chocolate Chip Cookie Dough, you may find yourself wondering if it's too much of a good thing. Well, this is what I have to say to that: the line between awful and awesome can be a fine one, and a lot of these sweet treats are best enjoyed in extreme moderation. No, I don't suggest eating Cadbury Creme Eggs Benedict or Deep-Fried Cupcakes on a Stick on a daily basis. But don't be scared, because a few bites won't kill you. Or if they do—what a way to go. Moreover, I strive to bring a sense of fun and fearlessness to baking, and I hope this book will inspire you to do the same.

WHAT ARE MY QUALIFICATIONS? OK, you've got me there. I am not a professional baker. I consider myself an "adventure baker," and do tend to approach my baking in a fairly lighthearted, laissez-faire way. I try to be unfussy when giving instructions to you, and I applaud your efforts to adapt or build upon these recipes to suit your equipment and taste preferences, but I have presented each recipe in the way that has reliably worked for me.

WHAT'S UP WITH THAT LITTLE CUPCAKE CHARACTER? Oh, I see you've noticed Cuppie, the CakeSpy mascot. Cuppie's story is that he (yes, it's a he) was made using a little bit of leftover cake batter, and as a result has always had a chip on his shoulder about not being his own complete cake. As a result, he is constantly trying to carve out his own little place in the world through adventures and misadventures, with a sense of mischief that is a hallmark of the CakeSpy sphere.

OK, now that we've covered the basics—let's get down to the business of making your life sweeter.

Breakfasts of Champions

SWEET STARTS TO THE DAY

Glazed Cinnamon Rolls
Stuffed with Chocolate Chip
Cookie Dough

Birthday Cake French Toast

Homemade Toaster Treats

Brunch Cookies

Trompe L'oeil Bagels with
Cream Cheese

Twice-Fried Doughnuts

Rolling Scones

Cadbury Creme Eggs
Benedict

Biscuits with Chocolate
Gravy

Glazed Cinnamon Rolls Stuffed with Chocolate Chip Cookie Dough

It's true: stuffing cinnamon rolls with chocolate chip cookie dough really does make them more delicious. I know this, because one serendipitous morning, I happened to be making cinnamon rolls while concurrently preparing some cookie dough for a Cookie Cake Pie (page 73). I suspected that there was a sweet possibility for recipe fusion here, and I was right: the resulting rolls were gooey, high-fat, high-carb heaven. While I use the pop-and-bake variety of cinnamon rolls, feel totally free to use your favorite home-made version.

8 ROLLS

1 package pop-and-bake cinnamon rolls with glaze

8 heaping tablespoons chocolate chip cookie dough, homemade or store-bought

Preheat the oven as directed on the cinnamon roll package.

Pull the paper tab on the package of cinnamon rolls until you get that festive "pop" that means the feast has been unleashed. Separate the rolls and gently unroll one of them.

On a separate work surface, roll a tablespoon of cookie dough into a thin log (using floured hands if the dough is sticky); it should be slightly narrower than the width of the cinnamon roll. Place the log of dough on top of the uncoiled dough, and gently re-roll. Repeat with the rest of the rolls.

Place the rolls on a lightly greased pie plate or 8-by-8-inch baking pan and bake according to the package directions.

Warm the packaged glaze in the microwave for about 10 seconds, or until pourable. Liberally glaze the cinnamon rolls and serve immediately.

Birthday Cake French Toast

Say hello to your new best friend: Birthday Cake French Toast. This recipe breathes new life into birthday cake (or any frosted layer cake, for that matter) that is past its prime. The cake's day-old dryness is perfect to absorb a rich, eggy mixture, and is then panfried (frosting and all) to yield a new breed of French toast that is beyond decadent. Of course, if you want to progress beyond the valley of decadence, why not drizzle the finished slices with a confectioners' sugar glaze and sprinkles?

3 TO 4 SERVINGS

4 large eggs

½ cup milk or heavy cream

3 tablespoons sugar

Dash of cinnamon, nutmeg, or cloves

2 to 4 tablespoons butter for frying

6 to 8 slices leftover birthday cake, chilled thoroughly in the refrigerator

Sprinkles, to garnish (optional)

In a large bowl, whisk the eggs, milk, sugar, and your choice of spices until the mixture is fully combined and lightly frothy.

In a large frying pan, melt 2 tablespoons of the butter over medium-high heat. When the butter is completely melted and lightly bubbling, you're ready to start frying the cake slices.

Remove the cake from the refrigerator (chilling it overnight keeps the frosting from melting when you fry the slices). Dip the first cake slice into the egg mixture, coating it completely. Place the dipped slice directly into the frying pan. Depending on the size of the pan, you can fry 2 or 3 slices at one time.

Let each slice fry for a minute or so, or until the sides are lightly rising up from the pan as the hot butter bubbles (you can lift a side gently with a spatula to see if it is browning). Turn the pieces over and cook on the other side, being sure to handle each one carefully so that the frosting doesn't smear across the pan. If the frosting does smear, don't panic; it will still taste good.

Transfer the slices to a serving platter or directly to plates. Repeat with the remaining slices, adding more butter as needed. If desired, top with a confectioners' sugar glaze and sprinkles. Serve immediately.

Homemade Toaster Treats

One of the biggest conflicts of my childhood had to do with the issue of Pop-Tarts versus Toaster Strudel. Those twin quasars of toaster awesomeness each had something to offer: one had sprinkles, but the other had little frosting packets that you could use to choose your own glazed adventure. These days, I prefer this homemade version, which is an adaptation of a recipe I originally found on the brilliant food blog Culinary Concoctions by Peabody. This version doesn't fare as well in the toaster, but it sure has a leg up on either commercial variety in the deliciousness department.

6 TO 8 PASTRIES

For the pastry:

1½ cups all-purpose flour

1 teaspoon salt

½ cup (1 stick) cold butter, cut into cubes (can use half shortening)

3 tablespoons cold milk

For the filling:

6 to 8 tablespoons jam, preserves, peanut butter, chocolate ganache, or other filling of your choice

For the icing:

1 cup confectioners' sugar, sifted

2 tablespoons milk or heavy cream, plus 1 to 2 tablespoons extra as needed

Sprinkles, to garnish

Preheat the oven to 450 degrees F. Line a baking sheet with parchment paper; set to the side.

Combine the flour and salt in a large bowl. Add the butter and cut it into the flour using two forks or a pastry cutter. Blend until the mixture resembles coarse crumbs. Add the milk bit by bit, gently mixing the dough after each addition, until the dough forms a ball (you may not need all of the milk).

Place dough on a lightly floured surface and roll it into a large rectangle about ⅛-inch thick. Cut out rectangles approximately the size of index cards (3 by 5 inches), or smaller if you prefer a more modest portion. Make sure you have an even number of cutouts.

Transfer half of the rectangles to your prepared baking sheet (If they are hard to handle, use a spatula to transfer the pieces).

On these rectangles, place a tablespoonful of your filling of choice in the center. Add a second rectangle on top of each piece, pressing down gently to spread the filling toward the edges.

Crimp all four edges with the tines of a fork to ensure that the filling doesn't ooze out. Poke the top of each with the fork to allow the steam to vent.

Bake for 7 to 9 minutes, or until light golden on the edges. Remove from the oven and let them cool completely.

While the pastries cool, prepare the icing: In a medium bowl, mix the confectioners' sugar with just enough cream to make a glaze that is thick but still pourable. Drizzle it over the pastries. Garnish with sprinkles immediately after drizzling with glaze.

Brunch Cookies

Cookies for brunch? Yes, please. This "kitchen sink" drop cookie includes all of the elements that make for a fantastic brunch: eggs, orange juice, bacon, and a touch of champagne (if you're that kind of bruncher). But don't for one moment confuse these with a savory breakfast pastry—they very much maintain the structure, taste, and crumb of a cookie. These simultaneously sweet, salty, and citrusy cookies won't be for everyone, but that's OK—more for you and me to enjoy as a one-stop brunch that you can munch on the go.

12 JUMBO COOKIES

¾ cup (1½ sticks) butter, softened

½ cup packed light brown sugar

1 large egg

1 tablespoon orange juice concentrate

1 tablespoon champagne (optional)

1¼ cups all-purpose flour

1 teaspoon baking powder

4 thick strips of bacon or veggie bacon, cooked until very crisp, crumbled into small pieces

½ cup small-piece cereal, such as Grape-Nuts, or larger-piece cereal, crushed into small pieces, or quick-cooking rolled oats

Coarse sea salt, to sprinkle on top of the cookies (optional)

Preheat the oven to 350 degrees F. Line two baking sheets with parchment paper and set to the side.

Beat the butter, sugar, egg, orange juice concentrate, and champagne in a medium bowl with an electric mixer at medium speed until light and fluffy.

Whisk the flour with the baking powder; add it to the butter mixture, beating on low speed until well blended. Stir in the bacon and cereal, mixing just until incorporated.

Using a large ice cream scoop (about ¼ cup per scoop), drop mounds of dough 3 inches apart onto the prepared baking sheets, to allow for spreading. If you don't have an ice cream scoop, you can also form large balls of dough (about 1½ inches in diameter) by hand. If you like an assertively salty cookie, sprinkle the tops of the balls of dough with some coarse sea salt directly before baking. Bake for 12 to 15 minutes, or until the edges are golden. Remove cookies from pans while still warm and cool them on wire racks.

Trompe L'oeil Bagels with Cream Cheese

This one's dedicated to all of you who have had friends or family (or both) accuse you of having a "problem" because you like to eat cake in the morning. It's not a problem. It's a habit. And you can trick them into thinking you're eating something savory instead of indulging your sweet tooth by constructing a frosting-filled doughnut topped with poppy seeds that looks exactly like a deliciously chock-full-of-carbohydrates bagel with cream cheese! When breakfast treats collide this sweetly, the awesome speaks for itself.

1 SERVING

1 plain cake doughnut

1 teaspoon butter, melted

Poppy seeds or sesame seeds for topping

1 generous dollop Vanilla Buttercream Frosting (page 50) or your favorite cream cheese frosting, at room temperature

Slice the doughnut horizontally in half.

In a small microwave-safe dish, melt the butter by heating it in the microwave for about 10 seconds. Using a pastry brush, lightly brush the top side of the doughnut with the melted butter (oh, get over it—they're already fried, anyway). Immediately sprinkle poppy seeds on top of the buttered halves. Some seeds will fall off, but enough will stick to give you the right effect.

Apply a generous dollop of frosting to the bottom half of the doughnut and gently spread it to the edges. Note: it's very important that the frosting be at room temperature, because if it is cold the doughnut may break apart when you try to spread it.

Put the poppy seed–laden piece on top and consume immediately. Not to boss you around or anything, but they taste great with coffee.

ceci n'est pas un bagel. · Quoi?

Twice-Fried Doughnuts

It's a fact: doughnuts fried twice are doubly nice. Not only is it a pleasing way to add more butter to your life, but it is also an effective way of bringing stale doughnuts back to life. This indulgent recipe is one I dreamed up in college, when inspiration for such dishes usually strikes late at night, when adding more butter always seems like a great idea, and when it's hard to discern whether you're eating a late night snack or an early morning breakfast.

1 doughnut, cake or yeast

1 tablespoon butter

2 tablespoons jam or preserves of choice

Gently slice the doughnut horizontally in half. In a frying pan large enough to accommodate the two doughnut halves at once, melt the butter over medium-high heat. When it starts to lightly bubble at the edges, place the doughnut halves in the pan, sliced side down.

After about a minute (when the edges of the doughnut are starting to brown) flip and let the other sides fry until lightly crispy. The second side won't need to fry as long as the first side. Remove from the frying pan and place on paper towels to blot any excess butter.

Spoon jam on top. Serve immediately.

Rolling Scones

Technically, these treats are more appropriate for brunch, because everyone knows that rock 'n' rollers never eat breakfast before noon. But no matter the hour you're waking up, what better way to pay homage (in pastry form) to one of the most influential rock bands of all time than with scones decorated to resemble their members? Complete with the slightest touch of brown sugar, these stones—I mean, scones—are cute and delicious enough that they'll gather no moss. Below you'll find my scone recipe—but really, you can use any scone recipe you like and skip right to the decorating section.

8 SCONES

For the scones:

2 cups all-purpose flour

¼ cup granulated sugar

¼ cup packed light brown sugar

1 tablespoon baking powder

½ teaspoon salt

6 tablespoons (¾ stick) butter, cold, cut into ½-inch cubes

1 cup heavy cream, cold

For the decoration:

Vanilla Buttercream Frosting (page 50)

Chocolate Fudge Buttercream Frosting (page 65) or Cocoa Buttercream Frosting (page 76)

Colored gel or writing icings and/or food-safe decorating markers

Preheat oven to 425 degrees F. Line a baking sheet with parchment paper.

Mix the flour, granulated sugar, light brown sugar, baking powder, and salt in a large bowl.

Add the butter cubes to the flour and sugar mixture. Cut it in using two forks, a pastry cutter, or your very clean hands, until the largest pieces are no bigger than a pea. Make a well in the center of this mixture and pour the cream into the well. Using your hands or a wooden spoon, mix quickly until the dry ingredients are all moistened. Gather the dough into a ball and place it on a lightly floured surface.

Knead the dough several times, pushing it with the heel of your hand and folding it over until the dough is smooth. Pat the ball into a 9-inch circle, ½- to ¾-inch thick. Cut into 8 wedges (like a pizza). Shape the wedges into ovals, making sure to pinch the middle to form a little bit of a nose and facial structure.

Place the scones on the baking sheet and bake for 15 minutes, or until golden brown and still slightly moist in the center.

Once cool, decorate each scone with dollops of frosting for hair (vanilla for the drummer, chocolate for the rest of the band) and draw in facial features with a food-safe marker or the decorating icings. Most importantly, be sure to make exaggerated red icing lips for the Mick Jagger scone.

Cadbury Creme Eggs Benedict

Eggs Benedict is like pleasure overload: savory little stacks of delicious excess topped with a crowning glory of Hollandaise sauce. But could this brunch classic be re-created in a totally sweet form? You bet your bottom silver dollar pancake. Picture this: it starts with an open-faced doughnut, followed by layers of brownie, melty Cadbury Creme Eggs (complete with oozing yolk!), and a topping of rich frosting, all accompanied by a mound of fried pound cake cubes that mimic a side of potatoes. It's time to say hello to a new classic.

CAKESPY NOTE: *While I realize that brownies might not have an accurate hue to represent the layer of ham, I chose them for their sturdy texture and for their deliciousness quotient. A pink cookie or layer of colored marzipan could be substituted if you really wanted a hammy look, though.*

2 SERVINGS

2 plain cake doughnuts

2 brownies (the fudgier the better)

¼ cup (½ stick) butter

2 slices pound cake, cut into small cubes

4 Cadbury Creme Eggs

¼ cup Vanilla Buttercream Frosting (page 50)

Red sugar sprinkles, to garnish

Slice the doughnuts horizontally into halves (the way you would slice a bagel); place two halves on each plate, cut side up.

Cut the brownies horizontally in half so that you have four full-size, thin brownie pieces. Cut each piece into a circle so that it is slightly smaller in circumference than the doughnut halves. Place the brownie circles on top of the doughnut halves. Set these partially constructed stacks to the side for the moment.

In a large frying pan, melt the butter over medium heat; add the cubed pound cake. Let the cake pieces fry for about 2 minutes or until crisp and browned on the edges, turning them at least once to ensure even browning. Place a mound of the fried cake cubes on the side of the plates not inhabited by the doughnut and brownie stacks.

Prepare the Creme Eggs. The idea is to get them lightly melty, but not so soft that the yolk oozes out. The best way to do this is to put them on a sheet of aluminum foil atop a baking pan and heat them in a moderately warm (about 350 degrees F) oven for about a minute. As soon as the chocolate on top of the eggs starts to get a bit shiny, remove them from the oven and very carefully transfer each egg to the top of each prepared brownie and doughnut stack.

Place 1 tablespoon of the buttercream frosting on top of each stack. If the eggs are still a bit warm, the buttercream should start to melt slightly, giving it the look of hollandaise sauce. If your buttercream is fairly stiff, you might consider lightly warming it in the microwave so that it is still thick but soft enough to be spooned prettily on top.

Sprinkle each finished stack with red sugar sprinkles to mimic the customary paprika garnish. Serve immediately.

Biscuits with Chocolate Gravy

Ever since I heard that it was one of Dolly Parton's favorite things to eat, I've been obsessed with the very idea of biscuits and chocolate gravy. I mean, seriously. It's like biscuits and gravy . . . but sweet! And happily, it's a food that is truly as delicious as it sounds. In my version, the chocolate gravy is basically a chocolate ganache liberally ladled over lightly sweetened biscuits. I'll warn you: this viscous, chocolatey mess might not be a beautiful dish to serve, but it sure is tasty. If you're in a rush, a thick chocolate fudge ice cream sauce will do as well.

6 SERVINGS (2 BISCUITS PER PERSON)

For the biscuits:

1¾ cups all-purpose flour

2 teaspoons baking powder

1 teaspoon salt

6 tablespoons (¾ stick) cold butter, cut into small pieces

¾ to 1 cup heavy cream

3 tablespoons butter, melted

For the chocolate gravy:

½ cup (1 stick) unsalted butter, cut into small pieces

1 cup heavy cream

16 ounces bittersweet chocolate, finely chopped

Preheat the oven to 450 degrees F. Prepare two baking sheets by lining them with parchment paper.

Sift the flour, baking powder, and salt into a large mixing bowl. Add the cold butter and cut it into the flour using a pastry cutter, two knives, or your fingertips until it forms pea-size clumps. Pour in ¾ cup of the cream; using either a wooden spoon or your hands, quickly combine the wet and dry ingredients. If the dough seems too dry, add the rest of the cream a few tablespoons at a time until it is cohesive.

Turn the dough out onto a floured surface. Knead it briefly with floured hands, then roll or pat out the dough until it is about ½ inch thick. Using a biscuit or cookie cutter that measures 2 to 3 inches in diameter, cut out biscuits and place them on the prepared baking sheets, leaving about an inch between biscuits to allow for slight expansion while baking.

Brush the tops of the biscuits with the melted butter (this is not the time for cutting calories), and bake for 10 to 15 minutes or until golden on top.

While the biscuits are baking, prepare the chocolate gravy. Heat the cream and butter in a deep saucepan over medium heat, stirring frequently, until the butter is completely melted. Remove the pan from the heat just before the mixture reaches the boiling point. Add the chopped chocolate and stir until it has melted.

Ladle a generous spoonful of chocolate gravy on top of each biscuit. Serve immediately.

Smart Cookies

IT'S ALL ABOUT THE COOKIE

Tiffany & Co. Bonbon
Cookies

S'moreos

Tele-Graham Crackers

Rainbow Cookies

Elvis Whoopie Pies

Blondie-Topped Brownies

Nanaimo Bars

Tricked-Out Cereal Treats

Chocolate Peanut Butter
Cereal Bars

Tiffany & Co. Bonbon Cookies

If Audrey Hepburn had been eating cookies instead of a croissant in the famous opening scene of Breakfast at Tiffany's, *I'd like to think that they would have looked like this: small, delicate bonbon cookies inspired by the famous jeweler's box hue. Of course, in cookie form, they're equally pleasant to eat as they are to behold.*

12 TO 14 COOKIES

For the cookies:

½ cup (1 stick) butter, softened

¾ cup confectioners' sugar, sifted

2 teaspoons vanilla extract

1½ cups all-purpose flour

¼ teaspoon salt

1 to 2 tablespoons heavy cream or milk (optional)

Food coloring in blue, yellow, and green

For the filling:

Choose your own adventure: I like chocolate chips, chopped nuts, or coconut

For the icing:

1 cup confectioners' sugar

2 tablespoons heavy cream or milk

Food coloring in blue, yellow, and green (do not use gel food coloring)

Pearl sugar or white sprinkles, to garnish

Heat the oven to 350 degrees F. Line a baking sheet with parchment paper.

Using an electric mixer, beat together the butter, confectioners' sugar, and vanilla until light and fluffy.

In a separate bowl, sift together the flour and salt. Slowly add the dry mixture to the sugar mixture, pausing to scrape down the sides of the bowl as needed. If your dough is too dry, add a teaspoon or two of milk or cream until it is easier to handle. Add the food coloring, mixing until no swirls of color are left. Note: to attain the perfect "blue box" color, I've found that 3 parts blue, 1 part green, and a dot of yellow coloring make a perfect faux-Tiffany hue.

Using an ice cream scoop or large spoon, wrap spoonfuls of dough around the filling of your choice, making sure that it is completely contained by dough. Form into balls about 1½ inches in diameter.

Place dough balls one inch apart on the baking sheet and bake for 12 to 15 minutes, or until the cookies have a dull finish on top. If you're not sure about doneness, lift one cookie up; the bottom should be lightly golden, not brown. Remove cookies from the oven and cool completely before frosting.

Prepare the icing. Mix the confectioners' sugar with just enough cream so that the icing is thick but still easily stirred. If desired, add food coloring to match or complement the cookies' hue.

Turn each cookie upside down and carefully dip the top of it into the icing. Immediately after dipping, sprinkle with your desired garnish.

S'moreos

Have you ever found yourself mid-s'more, feeling like maybe, just maybe, something is missing? Well, you're right. That missing thing is cream filling, and the solution can be found in a certain famous sandwich cookie called the Oreo. That's right: S'moreos! When s'mores meet Oreos, magic ensues—in the form of an oozy, creamy, unapologetically sugary morsel. Modesty aside, you won't be able to believe you've lived this long without a S'moreo.

CAKESPY NOTE: *I make mine in the microwave, as I am not the outdoorsy type; however, if there is a campfire handy, feel free to make yours using real toasted marshmallows.*

1 SERVING

1 or 2 Oreos (regular or Double Stuf), depending on how decadent you feel

2 chocolate rectangles from a regular-size Hershey's milk chocolate bar

Half a jumbo marshmallow per s'moreo (a whole one is just too big)

If you've elected to use just one Oreo, start by twisting it apart. Face the filled side up and put the chocolate squares on top, then add the marshmallow; top it off with the remaining Oreo half. Microwave on high for approximately 15 seconds. The marshmallow will puff and may cause the top half of the Oreo to fall off. This is OK—simply place it back on top of the S'moreo and enjoy immediately.

If you're going for the double Oreo version (good decision), repeat the same steps as above, simply using a whole Oreo for the top and bottom pieces. It may take a few more seconds in the microwave, but it's oh so worth it.

Tele-Graham Crackers

Although CakeSpy Headquarters is in Seattle, I am originally from a magical place known as New Jersey; as such, I am often seeking sweet treats that can handle being indelicately tumbled by the postal service while retaining their essential goodness. By far the simplest—and cleverest—solution I've ever come up with is the Tele-Graham Cracker. When these sweet little treats arrive in the mail, you'll give a shout-out to the lost art of communication and offer sweet (or not so sweet) greetings.

12 TELE-GRAHAM CRACKERS

12 graham crackers

2 cups frosting, such as Vanilla Buttercream Frosting (page 50), or another filling (peanut butter or Nutella both work nicely)

Writing icing, such as Cake Mate Writing Icing Decorator Tubes (tubes marked "Gel Icing" will not work as they do not harden!)

Small boxes (jewelry boxes, available at most craft or packaging supply stores, work nicely)

Padded mailers or shipping boxes

Break each graham cracker in half so that you have two square pieces.

Spread your filling on one side of each pair and adhere the second half on top to form a little sandwich.

Using your writing icing, write your message on the top of the cookie.

> **NEED A SUGGESTION?** Aside from the expected "Miss You" or "Wish You Were Here," these tele-grahams provide a great opportunity to make your more complex thoughts known in a sugar-coated way. "None of Us Likes Your Boyfriend, Please Break Up with Him," "Why Don't You Move Out of Your Parents' Basement?" and "Nice Nose Job" would all be appropriate. Or not.

Let dry; once the icing is set, wrap in waxed paper and place in small boxes (I find that 3½-inch square jewelry boxes work nicely; they're available at Uline .com or at packaging supply stores). Use crinkled paper to fill the top and bottom of the boxes, and all of those in a padded mailer or box. These confections will fare well for 3 to 4 days, so choose your method of shipping accordingly.

 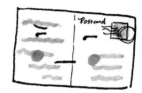

Rainbow Cookies

Sure, you could get a sweet thrill from checking out the pretty patterns in a kaleido-scope. But it's much more delicious to taste the rainbow—delivered via crumbly, but-tery, colorful cookies. This is based on a retro recipe I fell in love with at a craft fair in Portland, where Sara Bir served a similar cookie to go with her boyfriend Joe's colorful rainbow tape art. Divide the dough into as many or as few color segments as you'd like, creating a unique palette that appeals to your palate.

60 TO 70 SMALL COOKIES

1 pound (4 sticks) unsalted butter, softened

2 cups confectioners' sugar, sifted

½ teaspoon salt

2 teaspoons vanilla extract

4½ cups all-purpose flour

Food coloring in various colors

Sprinkles or colored decorating sugar, to garnish (about 1 cup)

In an electric stand mixer, beat the butter with a paddle attachment until it is creamy. Starting on the lowest speed, add the confectioners' sugar and salt and beat for several minutes, until all of the ingredients are well incorporated. Beat in the vanilla, then add the flour in 3 to 4 additions, scraping down the sides of the bowl after each addition, and mix until a soft dough forms.

Turn the dough out onto a lightly floured surface and divide it into as many parts as you want to have colors. Add the food coloring of your choosing to each portion of dough—be sure to make the colors quite vibrant, as they will fade slightly in the oven. Knead until the colors are evenly distributed.

Roll each tinted segment into a log about a foot long. Then squish all the colored logs together so that they form one roll (it will be quite large in circumference). Gently roll so that the various colors of dough stick together; you don't need to worry too much about the colors coming together irregularly, because you will ultimately get a nice, wavy design when you cut the cookies out.

Cut the log of dough with all of the colors combined in half, so that you have two logs of dough; re-roll each log again until it has reached a circumference of about 1½ to 2 inches. These may be quite long, so you might want to slice them into several shorter logs for easy storage. If desired, place the sprinkles or decorating sugar on a large, shallow plate and roll each log to coat. Wrap the logs in parchment or wax paper and refrigerate until the dough is completely chilled (or freeze for up to a month).

When you're ready to bake, preheat the oven to 375 degrees F.

Unwrap the chilled logs and, with a sharp knife, slice them into coins about ⅓ inch thick. (If the dough is still frozen, let it warm up just enough to slice easily; don't let it get so soft that it's hard to handle.)

Place on baking sheets, leaving about an inch between cookies (they will spread a little during baking). Bake two sheets at a time for 7 to 9 minutes, rotating the pans halfway through baking, until the cookies have firmed up but are not browned. Let cool on the sheet for about 5 minutes, then transfer the cookies to a wire rack to cool completely.

Elvis Whoopie Pies

What is an Elvis Whoopie Pie? A hunka hunka burnin' yum, that's what. Comprised of two fat, cakey banana cookies sandwiched with a lavish amount of honey-peanut butter buttercream, these substantial treats are then studded along the sides with bits of bacon, forming a sweet and salty masterpiece that will satisfy even king-size appetites. This is a recipe I originally developed for New York City's Peanut Butter & Co., which I strongly believe makes the best peanut butter in the world.

12 KING-SIZE WHOOPIE PIES

For the cookies:
1 cup (2 sticks) butter, softened

1 cup packed light brown sugar

2 large eggs

2 large (or 3 small) very ripe bananas, mashed

½ cup milk

1 teaspoon vanilla

3 cups all-purpose flour

1½ teaspoons baking soda

1 teaspoon salt

For the filling:
1 cup (2 sticks) butter, softened

3 to 4 cups confectioners' sugar, sifted

¾ cup smooth peanut butter, preferably Peanut Butter & Co.® The Bee's Knees®

1 teaspoon vanilla extract

4 to 6 teaspoons heavy cream

For the garnish (optional):
1 to 2 strips thick-cut bacon, cooked until very crisp, crumbled into small pieces

Make the cookies. In a stand mixer fitted with the paddle attachment, cream the butter and sugar until fluffy and light. Add the eggs, one at a time, mixing well after each addition. Add the bananas, milk, and vanilla, and mix on low speed until incorporated.

In a separate bowl, whisk the flour, baking soda, and salt; beat in, bit by bit, until the mixture is fully combined. Chill the dough for 1 to 2 hours in the refrigerator.

Preheat the oven to 375 degrees F. Line two baking sheets with parchment paper.

Using a large (¼ cup) ice cream scoop, drop rounds of dough onto the baking sheets, leaving at least 2 inches between cookies. You should be able to fit six cookies on each pan.

Bake for about 10 minutes, or until lightly browned on the edges. Let cool completely on a wire rack before filling.

While the cookies cool, prepare the filling. In a stand mixer fitted with the paddle attachment, cream the butter and 3 cups of the confectioners' sugar until light and fluffy. Add peanut butter and vanilla and continue to beat until very fluffy. Pour in 4 teaspoons of the heavy cream and stir until completely incorporated. The consistency should be like a fairly stiff buttercream frosting; if it does not seem firm enough, add the remaining cup of confectioners' sugar, bit by bit, until you have achieved your desired consistency. If needed to attain an ideal consistency, add the remaining heavy cream.

Spoon a healthy dollop of peanut butter frosting on one overturned cookie half and put another on top to sandwich. Do not press too hard or your filling will squeeze out the sides—and trust me, you don't want to lose one blessed bit.

Lightly sprinkle bacon bits on the frosted edges; a small amount per pie really does go a long way. Serve immediately after adding the bacon, as the bacon flavor does get more powerful the longer they sit, and this can be a bit much for some eaters.

Blondie-Topped Brownies

Blondies or brownies? It's a delicious dilemma: they're both bar cookie classics, one rich in brown sugar, the other redolent of chocolate. But why should you have to decide when they taste so much better baked together? True: This recipe is a bit of a labor of love, because blondies and brownies generally require different baking times. However, once you try a bite of these tasty two-layered treats, I'm sure you'll agree it's worth the effort.

24 TO 36 SERVINGS

For the brownie layer:

1¼ cups unsweetened cocoa powder

1¼ cups all-purpose flour

½ teaspoon salt

1½ cups (3 sticks) unsalted butter, melted

3 cups sugar

5 large eggs

2 teaspoons vanilla extract

For the blondie layer:

⅔ cup unsalted butter, melted

2 cups packed dark brown sugar

2 large eggs, lightly beaten

2 teaspoons vanilla extract

2 cups all-purpose flour

1 teaspoon baking powder

1 teaspoon salt

One 12-ounce bag semisweet chocolate chips (optional)

1 cup chopped nuts (optional)

Preheat the oven to 375 degrees F.

Generously grease the bottom and sides of a 3-quart, 9-by-13-inch baking pan.

First, make the brownie layer. In a medium mixing bowl, combine the cocoa powder, flour, and salt; sift together and set aside.

To the bowl of a stand mixer fitted with the paddle attachment, add the melted butter and sugar; starting on a slow speed, beat them together until they form a cohesive, slightly gritty mixture.

Beat in the eggs one at a time, pausing to scrape down the sides of the bowl after each addition. Continue beating on medium speed until the mixture reaches a creamy consistency and is light yellow in color. Beat in the vanilla. Add the dry mixture, bit by bit, beating on low speed and continuing to scrape down the sides of the bowl until well blended. Pour the batter into the prepared pan and spread it evenly.

Bake for 20 minutes. The brownies will just be beginning to set at this point, so don't be alarmed if they are still jiggly in the center.

While the brownies bake, prepare the blondie batter. If the brownies have finished baking before you are done preparing the blondie batter, simply set the brownies to the side; leave the oven on, but reduce heat to 350 degrees F.

Clean the mixing bowl and paddle. Add the melted butter and brown sugar to the bowl and mix on low speed until smooth. Beat in the eggs one at a time, scraping the bowl between additions. Add the vanilla and continue beating on medium speed until the batter is smooth and fluffy.

Combine the flour, baking powder, and salt in a large bowl.

Add the flour mixture bit by bit, mixing well and making sure to scrape down the sides of the bowl occasionally. Fold in the chocolate chips and nuts last, by hand; the batter will be fairly thick.

Gently spoon the blondie batter on top of the partially baked brownies. Because the brownies are at a fragile stage, it works best if you gently ladle the blondie batter on top of the brownie batter (never actually touching the brownie batter with a spatula or spoon, but letting it drip onto the layer) as evenly as you can, rather than trying to spread it with a spatula. It's OK if you can still see a bit of brownie peeking out here and there, but you want the top to be mostly covered with blondie batter.

Put the pan back in the oven for 30 to 40 minutes, or until the blondie layer is beginning to brown on the edges and has a dull finish on top, and a toothpick inserted in the center comes out mostly clean. Let them cool in the pan; you might even consider refrigerating them for a few hours so that they can set up properly before cutting and serving.

Nanaimo Bars

Forget hockey, maple syrup, and Alanis Morisette: Nanaimo Bars are, hands down, the best thing that Canada has ever given the world. These no-bake bars, comprised of a chocolate-crumb crust, a custardy middle layer and a crowning glory of firm chocolate topping, have hazy origins. (Were they invented by a Nanaimo housewife as a blue-ribbon baking contest entry? Or are they an adaptation of something called the New York Slice?) One thing's certain, though: these decadent treats are dangerously addictive.

36 SMALL BARS

For the bottom layer:

½ cup (1 stick) butter

¼ cup sugar

5 tablespoons unsweetened cocoa powder

1 large egg, beaten

1½ cups graham cracker crumbs

½ cup finely chopped nuts (preferably walnuts, pecans, or almonds)

1 cup shredded sweetened coconut

NANAIMO BAR ♥

For the middle layer:

½ cup (1 stick) butter

2 tablespoons heavy cream

2 tablespoons custard powder, such as Bird's, but if you can't find that, 2 tablespoons vanilla instant pudding powder works

2 cups confectioners' sugar, sifted

For the top layer:

Four 1-ounce squares bittersweet or semisweet chocolate, coarsely chopped

1½ tablespoons butter

Line the bottom of an 8-inch square baking pan with parchment paper or foil for easy removal of the bars from the pan once they are done.

Prepare the bottom layer: Melt the butter, sugar, and cocoa powder in a double boiler. Add the beaten egg and stir vigorously with a wooden spoon until incorporated and thick. Remove the pan from the heat, transfer to a large bowl, and stir in the graham cracker crumbs, nuts, and coconut. Press firmly into the prepared pan. Put this in the refrigerator for about half an hour so that it can set before you add the next layer.

Prepare the middle layer: In a stand mixer fitted with the paddle attachment, cream the butter, cream, custard powder, and confectioners' sugar until very light and fluffy. Spread over the bottom layer, taking care to spread it as flat and evenly as possible. Return the pan to the refrigerator while you prepare the topping.

Prepare the top layer: In a medium saucepan or double boiler, melt the chocolate and butter over medium heat, stirring often to ensure that the mixture doesn't scorch. Once the chocolate is completely smooth, remove the pan from the heat and set it aside to cool. Stir occasionally until the mixture is still liquid but very thick, then pour it over the middle layer and gently spread it with a spatula to ensure even coverage (work carefully, because the still-warm chocolate will get messy if you press too hard and tear up the buttery layer below).

Refrigerate for at least an hour before cutting into bars. To ensure clean slices, run a knife under hot water, dry with a cloth, then cut into the bars, cleaning the knife with a paper towel frequently between slices.

BAR IN NANAIMO♥

While the classic Nanaimo Bar is a pretty perfect food, here are some variations that you might enjoy.

PEANUT BUTTER NANAIMO BARS: Add ½ cup creamy peanut butter to the middle layer for a treat that will make peanut butter cups jealous.

CEREAL TREAT NANAIMO BARS: Instead of using the graham cracker bottom layer, use a batch of the base part of the Chocolate Peanut Butter Cereal Bars recipe (page 42), making for a crunchy and impossibly rich variation.

ROCKY ROAD NANAIMO BARS: Add ¾ cup mini-marshmallows and small shards of graham crackers to the chocolate topping immediately after removing it from the heat. Stir only until incorporated, and spoon this gooey, messy mixture on top of the bars.

BOOZY NANAIMO BARS: In the middle layer, substitute Bailey's Irish Cream for the heavy cream and Kahlua for the vanilla extract. Enjoy in moderation.

HOLIDAY PEPPERMINT NANAIMO BARS: Instead of vanilla extract, use peppermint in the middle layer, and add a teaspoon of peppermint extract to the top layer, too. Use green food coloring, if desired, for the middle custard layer.

HOLIDAY EGGNOG NANAIMO BARS: Instead of cream, use eggnog in the middle layer, and instead of bittersweet or semisweet chocolate, use 4 ounces of melted white chocolate for the top layer. Garnish with finely chopped nuts, cinnamon, and nutmeg.

Tricked-Out Cereal Treats

It's already been established that Rice Krispies are not the only cereal treat on the sweet circuit. But for the most sacchariferous and certainly the prettiest alternative, why not try a rainbow-hued cereal? You can then create some double rainbow magic by slicing your tutti-frutti-toned tidbits and stuffing them with frosting and sprinkles. If you are what you eat, than eaters of these treats are colorful, rich, and absolutely fabulous.

12 JUMBO OR 24 BITE-SIZE TREATS

3 tablespoons butter

4 cups miniature marshmallows

6 cups rainbow-hued cereal, such as Trix

2 cups Vanilla Buttercream Frosting (page 50)

Rainbow sprinkles, to garnish

Generously grease a 9-by-13-inch pan.

In a large saucepan, melt the butter over low heat. Add the marshmallows and stir until completely melted. Remove from heat. Add the cereal. Stir with a wooden spoon until well coated.

Spoon this sticky mixture into the prepared pan, pressing down with either clean, slightly wet fingers or the back of the spoon to make sure it is evenly and firmly packed into the pan. Set aside.

Let the treats cool completely, then cut into squares of any size you'd like.

Using a very sharp knife, cut the squares in half horizontally (like a bagel). Apply a liberal dollop of frosting to the bottom half, then top with the other half to form a sandwich. Apply rainbow sprinkles to the exposed frosting on the edges to really trick out your treats.

Chocolate Peanut Butter Cereal Bars

To me, the American Midwest is a magical land where bars reign supreme. I'm not talking about places where people meet and drink (although there are plenty of those, too). I'm talking about bar cookies. And one that fascinates me in particular, that I saw all over the place in South Dakota, is this variation of the old-fashioned cereal treat, that eschews marshmallows in favor of a peanut butter and corn syrup binder, and a thick topping of chocolate. These bars are almost indescribably rich, but completely addictive—so bad, but so good.

16 TO 24 SERVINGS

1½ cups packed light brown sugar

1¼ cups light corn syrup

2 cups peanut butter (a creamy, no-stir type works best)

6 cups flaked cereal (preferably Special K)

One 12-ounce bag semisweet chocolate chips

Generously grease a 9-by-13-inch pan.

In a large, microwave-safe bowl, combine the brown sugar and corn syrup; mix well. Microwave this mixture on high at one-minute intervals, for a total of about 4 minutes, removing the bowl and stirring the mixture after each minute. As you stir, scrape down the sides of the bowl. Once the mixture starts to bubble around the edges, carefully remove it from the microwave.

Add 1½ cups of the peanut butter; stir until smooth and fully incorporated. Do this gently, because you will have a fairly hot mixture on your hands, and getting splashed with that hot sugar mixture would be no fun, trust me. Add the cereal and mix with a wooden spoon or a heat-proof spatula until the cereal is completely coated.

Spoon this sticky mixture into the prepared pan, pressing down with either clean, slightly wet fingers or the back of the spoon to make sure it is evenly and firmly packed into the pan. Set aside.

In a medium microwave-safe bowl, combine the chocolate chips and the remaining ½ cup peanut butter. Heat on medium power for 30-second intervals until the chocolate begins to melt. When the chocolate chips are mostly melted, remove from the microwave and stir the mixture; the residual heat should melt the remaining chips. Stir until smooth, then spread on top of the cereal mixture. The chocolate mixture will become firm, but will not become completely hard.

Let cool completely and cut into bars. (Do not chill the mixture before cutting, as both the cereal mixture and the chocolate will harden and make it difficult to make neat edges.)

Taking the Cake

CAKES TO MAKE YOU LICK THE PLATE CLEAN

Grilled Cheesecake

Doughnut Upside-Down Cake

7-Up, Up, and Away Cake

Rainbow Layer Cake

Salad Dressing Cake

Cakes Baked in Jars

Behemoth Crumb Cake

Cupcake-Stuffed Cupcakes

Cupcakes Stuffed with
Chocolate Chip Cookie Dough

Cupcakes Baked in
Ice Cream Cones

Whoopie Pie Cupcakes

Grilled Cheesecake

Grilled cheese is pretty much the best thing since sliced bread. After all, it is sliced bread—with the added awesomeness of cheese and butter. Can it really get any better? After being hit with what can only be described as a stroke of pure genius, I can definitively say yes. It can get better. I'm talking, of course, about the grilled cheesecake sandwich. Made out of slivered cheesecake layered between slices of buttered pound cake, this sandwich is serious, all right—as serious as a heart attack.

1 SERVING

1 tablespoon butter

2 slices pound cake (any flavor), each piece buttered on one side

1 small slice cheesecake (any flavor), cut into very thin slices

Place the butter in a frying pan over medium heat and let it melt.

Assemble the sandwich as follows: one slice pound cake (buttered side down), as many slivers of cheesecake as you'd like (I include bits with the crust, too), and the other slice of pound cake, buttered side up.

Place the sandwich in the frying pan, still over medium heat. After about 1½ minutes, gently lift with a spatula to see if the sandwich is browned on the bottom. Once it is browned to your liking, carefully flip the sandwich. Gently press down on the top with the spatula to make everything meld together. The second side will brown faster than the first one, so keep a close eye on it.

Remove from the heat and slice the sandwich in half. Enjoy.

> **SERVING NOTE:** For those of you who simply can't eat a grilled cheese without soup, I think a bowl of slightly melty strawberry ice cream would complement this version quite nicely.

Doughnut Upside-Down Cake

Trying to improve a classic can be tricky business. However, when it comes to pineapple upside-down cake, I believe I may have actually done it—by transforming it into a cake that features our dear friend, the doughnut. How did I create this magic? I simply studied a classic recipe and replaced every instance of "pineapple" with "doughnut." Then I replaced shortening and milk with butter and heavy cream, respectively. The result, scientifically speaking? Holey yum.

12 TO 16 SERVINGS

½ cup (1 stick) butter

⅔ cup packed dark brown sugar

18 to 24 mini-doughnuts, plain or sugar coated

1⅓ cups all-purpose flour

1 cup granulated sugar

1½ teaspoons baking powder

½ teaspoon salt

⅓ cup butter, softened

¾ cup heavy cream

1 large egg

Heat the oven to 325 degrees F.

In a 9-by-13-inch pan, melt the butter in the oven while it is preheating. Remove the pan from the oven and sprinkle the brown sugar evenly over the melted butter. Arrange the mini-doughnuts in rows on top of the brown sugar.

In the bowl of an electric mixer fitted with the paddle attachment, beat the remaining ingredients on low speed for about 30 seconds. Scrape down the sides of the bowl, then beat on high speed for about 3 minutes, scraping bowl occasionally. Spoon the batter, which will be fairly thick, gently over the dough-nuts so as not to disturb their careful arrangement. The batter should cover the doughnuts, but you will still see their shape underneath.

Bake for 50 to 55 minutes, or until a toothpick inserted in the center of the cake comes out clean. Immediately place a large heatproof serving plate upside down over the cake pan; carefully flip the plate and pan over. Leave the pan in place for a few minutes so that the brown sugar mixture can drizzle over the cake, then lift the pan off. This cake is best when served warm, or the same day that it's baked.

VARIATION: Turn your leftover Hanukkah *Sufganiyot* (jelly-filled doughnuts) upside down—literally—simply substituting the jelly-filled doughnuts for the mini ones in this recipe. Since Sufganiyot are usually larger, use only as many whole doughnuts as you can fit in the pan; do not cut them in half or the jelly will get messy.

7-Up, Up, and Away Cake

While this cake gets its lift from buoyant lemon-lime soda bubbles, it's far from light-as-air. This is actually a rich, decadent pound cake made with three sticks of butter. Want to make it even more heavenly? Coloring the cake a gentle sky blue and topping it with a fluffy, cloud-like coating of rich coconut frosting lends an air of sweet drama when you slice into the cake.

12 SERVINGS

1½ cups (3 sticks) butter, softened

3 cups sugar

5 large eggs

3 cups all-purpose flour

2 teaspoons lemon juice

¾ cup lemon-lime soda

4 cups Vanilla Buttercream Frosting (recipe follows)

3 cups sweetened shredded coconut, to garnish

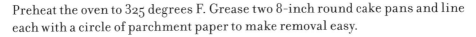

Preheat the oven to 325 degrees F. Grease two 8-inch round cake pans and line each with a circle of parchment paper to make removal easy.

In the bowl of a stand mixer fitted with the paddle attachment, cream the butter and sugar on low speed for 20 minutes. Yes, 20 minutes. Add the eggs, one at a time, beating until each is incorporated; pause occasionally to scrape down the sides of the bowl.

Gradually add the flour, bit by bit, until fully incorporated, once again scraping down the sides of the bowl as necessary. Add the lemon extract and lemon-lime soda. Finally, if desired, add a couple drops of blue food coloring (make the color a couple shades more vibrant than you want the final product, because it will fade a bit during baking) and mix until the ingredients are well combined.

Fill the two cake pans equally with batter. Bake the cakes side by side in the oven for 45 to 55 minutes, or until a toothpick inserted in the center of each cake comes out clean. Let cool completely before frosting.

To frost, first cut the tops of the cakes horizontally to level them, if necessary. Frost the bottom layer and then place the top layer on top of it, pressing very gently to help the layers adhere. Frost the rest of the cake, applying a crumb coat if needed (although the coconut garnish is quite forgiving if you have a crumb or two showing). Immediately after frosting the cake, pat the coconut onto the top and sides so that it adheres to the frosting and completely covers the cake, giving it a cloudlike, "up, up and away" appearance.

WHY CREAM THE BUTTER AND SUGAR FOR 20 MINUTES IN THIS RECIPE? Think of it this way: those little granules of sugar are like little knives cutting air pockets in the butter. Later on, all of these little pockets are going to be perfectly primed to receive the rest of the ingredients, so that the resulting cake is light and yet still decadently buttery.

VANILLA BUTTERCREAM FROSTING

4 CUPS FROSTING

2 sticks (1 cup) unsalted butter, softened

6 to 8 cups confectioners' sugar, sifted

¼ cup heavy cream

2 teaspoons vanilla extract

In the stand mixer with the paddle attachment, mix the butter on medium speed until it is very fluffy. Add 4 cups of the confectioners' sugar, and mix on low speed until smooth and incorporated. Pause to scrape down the sides of the bowl, and add the cream and vanilla. Beat on medium speed until smooth and creamy, 3 to 5 minutes, continuing to add sugar until it has reached your desired consistency. If your frosting becomes too stiff, you can thin it by adding more cream, but be careful to add the cream in small (teaspoon) increments so that the frosting does not become too thin.

Rainbow Layer Cake

If you truly want a dramatic dessert that will wow eaters of all ages, this is it. A six-layer cake in all the colors of the rainbow, this one is dramatic to cut into and always seems to elicit an "oooooooh" response. It is impossible to be unhappy while eating this cake. Special thanks go to Karen of the blog, off the (meat)hook, whose pictures of a similar cake inspired me to create this recipe.

2 batches vanilla cake batter, homemade or from a mix
Food coloring in red, orange, yellow, green, blue, and violet
8 cups Vanilla Buttercream Frosting (page 50)

Preheat the oven as specified in your cake recipe. Line six round cake pans (8- or 9-inch) with circles of parchment paper. If you don't have six pans (it's OK, neither do I), line as many as you have; you can bake this in a few batches.

Prepare the cake batter as specified in your recipe, but at the point when you would pour the batter into the pans, instead divide it between six separate bowls. Add food coloring to each of the bowls of batter: red, orange, yellow, green, blue, and violet. Be very liberal with the food coloring, as the colors will fade slightly during baking.

Pour the batter into the prepared pans and bake. Since these cakes are very thin, keep an eye on the baking time—it will be significantly less than for the normal layers.

Once baked, remove the cakes from the pans and set them on wire racks to cool.

Using a large knife (preferably serrated), slice the tops of the cakes to make them level. Place the violet layer on a serving plate and top with a dollop of frosting. Do not spread it to the edges, as the weight of the succeeding layers will flatten the frosting. Repeat with the remaining layers until they are stacked from bottom to top: violet, blue, green, yellow, orange, and red on top.

To stabilize the cake, place 2 to 3 long skewers down through it (just don't forget to remove them from the slices when served!). Chill the cake for at least 20 minutes; it will help it firm up and be easier to frost. Using an offset spatula, apply a thin crumb coat of frosting to all of the cake surfaces. Return the cake to the refrigerator for about 30 minutes so that the crumb coat becomes firm.

Remove from the refrigerator and apply the rest of the frosting. Keep the cake chilled until 30 minutes before serving.

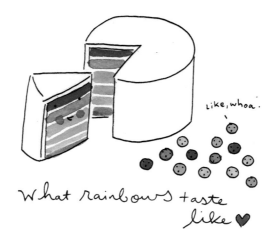

Like, whoa.

What rainbows taste like ♥

Salad Dressing Cake

Now, the name "Salad Dressing Cake" can be misleading—this is not some sort of exotic balsamic-glazed confection. No sir, the dressing we're talking about here is the one that dresses salads of the potato and macaroni varieties: you may know it as mayonnaise. I know, the initial reaction is to be grossed out. But just think about it: the makeup of mayonnaise—mainly egg yolks and oil—is all stuff that would go into a cake anyway. And the cake that you get when you use mayonnaise is remarkably moist and rich (just don't tell eaters what the secret ingredient is).

16 SERVINGS

2 cups all-purpose flour

2 teaspoons baking soda

1 cup sugar

¼ cup unsweetened cocoa powder

1 cup warm water

1 cup mayonnaise

1 teaspoon vanilla extract

2 cups frosting of your choice (optional)

Preheat the oven to 350 degrees F. Grease a 9-by-9-inch pan and dust it with flour.

In the bowl of a stand mixer fitted with the paddle attachment, mix all of the ingredients together (except the frosting), beating until smooth.

Pour the batter into the prepared pan and bake for 30 minutes, or until a toothpick inserted in the center comes out clean. Top with your choice of frosting after the cake has cooled.

Cakes Baked in Jars

If you really want to see something horrifying, try shipping a cupcake. Trust me, it's not pretty. However, if you want to share some sweetness with friends and family who may be far away, there is a solution: bake your cakes in jars. Yup, that's right: bake up your favorite cake or cupcake recipe directly in jars for contained, easy-to-ship parcels that can be topped with whipped cream or frosting when they've reached their destination. You will be remembered fondly for this thoughtful and tasty surprise.

CAKESPY NOTE: *I generally don't suggest frosting the cakes before shipping (unless it's a very short transit), but you can frost or top them and then put the lids on for short-term transit (for instance, if they're packed in a lunch).*

TWELVE TO FIFTEEN 8-OUNCE JAR SERVINGS

1 batch of your favorite cake batter, homemade or from a mix

Twelve to fifteen 8-ounce wide-mouth jars with lids (often called "pint-size" jars)

Wax paper, cut into circles slightly smaller than the circumference of the jar's mouth

Generously grease the bottom and inside surfaces of your clean jars. Preheat the oven as specified in your recipe, then prepare the cake batter according to the recipe's instructions.

When the cake batter is ready, spoon or pour it into the jars, filling them about halfway full (you want room to top them later!). Place them on a baking sheet. If your recipe baking time is for a whole cake, check these about 10 minutes sooner, as the smaller servings may reduce baking time. Insert a toothpick or skewer into the jar; when it comes out clean, the cakes are done.

Remove from the oven and let cool completely. Place a circle of wax paper on top of each cake to keep it from sticking to the top of the jar, and then place the lids on the jars.

To serve, slide a knife around the inside of the jar to loosen the cake; shake gently to remove it from the jar. You can also eat the cakes straight from the jar, but rest assured that either way, they're far tastier when topped with frosting or freshly whipped cream right before serving.

WHILE YOU CAN BAKE virtually any cupcake or cake recipe in glass jars, I find that moist, dense cakes tend to keep best during shipping. When it comes to the jars you use, you can choose your own adventure. I favor 8-ounce jars, but you can also use pint jars for larger cakes, or baby food jars for baby cakes. The key is to use jars with a fairly wide mouth, so that the cake can be removed easily. Also note that the baking time might be longer or shorter depending on the size of jar you use.

Behemoth Crumb Cake

When it comes to crumb topping, I have a theory: if some is good, more is better. And if I really look deep into my heart, what I want is roughly 90 percent crumb, 10 percent cake. My method? Take a crumb cake recipe and make it even better by halving the cake part and tripling the crumb part. The result? A hulking behemoth of crumb, anchored by a little sliver of cake.

36 SMALL SERVINGS

For the crumb topping:

3 cups (6 sticks) salted butter, softened

7½ cups all-purpose flour

4½ cups packed dark brown sugar

5 tablespoons ground cinnamon

4 teaspoons vanilla extract

For the cake:

1 cup all-purpose flour, sifted

2 teaspoons baking powder

¼ teaspoon salt

⅛ teaspoon baking soda

¼ cup (½ stick) butter, cut into small cubes

½ cup granulated sugar

1 large egg

½ teaspoon vanilla extract

⅓ cup sour cream

To make the topping, first melt the butter in a medium-large saucepan over low heat. Remove from the heat and cool for about five minutes, or until the butter is beginning to become slightly solid again. Do not allow it to become cold. Transfer the butter to a very large mixing bowl.

Add the flour, brown sugar, cinnamon, and vanilla. This is a very large amount to mix, so you'll either want to use your hands or large salad forks to mix it all together (two small forks or a pastry cutter simply aren't going to cut it!). Keep mixing until the butter is evenly distributed and the mixture forms into crumbs when pressed together. Set aside.

Preheat the oven to 350 degrees F.

Butter a 9-by-13-inch baking pan. Dust the pan lightly with flour.

Combine the flour, baking powder, salt, and baking soda in a large bowl, whisking to incorporate. Set aside.

In the bowl of a stand mixer fitted with the paddle attachment (or an electric hand mixer), cream the butter on medium speed until light, about 2 minutes. Add the sugar to the butter, and continue mixing on medium speed for about 2 more minutes. Scrape the sides of the bowl occasionally. Add the egg and vanilla, and continue mixing on medium speed, pausing and scraping the sides of the bowl as necessary.

Reduce the mixer speed to low. Add the dry ingredients alternately with the sour cream, starting and ending with the flour. Mix just until incorporated after each addition. Scrape the sides of the bowl as necessary and mix until you have a cohesive, smooth batter.

Turn the batter into the prepared pan, smoothing the surface with the back of a large spoon or rubber spatula. The batter will be very thinly spread and will just barely cover the bottom of the pan.

Take a handful of the crumb mixture and make a fist to press the mixture into a large clump. Then separate into smaller clusters, scattering them on top of the cake

nothin' but crumb.

batter. Repeat until all of the topping mixture has been used. Try to make sure that every surface of the cake batter is covered, as it will bubble up in any gaps you leave uncovered.

Set the pan on top of a baking sheet (to catch any overflow). Bake for 35 to 40 minutes, or until the crumbs are golden brown on top and the cake begins to come away from the sides of the pan. Remove from the oven and let cool completely before cutting and serving.

CAKESPY NOTE: You may notice that the cake feels fairly heavy. Curious, I weighed it before putting it in the oven. It weighed almost 11 pounds. Granted, this is including the weight of the Pyrex baking dish, but still pretty hefty, no?

Cupcake-Stuffed Cupcakes

I hold this truth to be self-evident: cupcakes are better when filled. This is a life lesson I learned from my dear friend Megan Seling, who blogs under the name Bake It in a Cake; there she bakes any- and everything you could dream of inside of cakes. But I've come up with the ultimate cupcake-stuffer: cupcakes themselves. By embedding miniature cupcakes—frosting and all—inside standard cupcake tins filled with batter, you get a surprisingly delightful treat. The mini-cupcakes, sealed by the moisture of the cake batter, don't dry out, and the baked bit of frosting lightly spreads, browns, and adds a rich crunch, making for an overall taste and visual contrast that can't be beat.

18 TO 24 SERVINGS

18 to 24 frosted miniature cupcakes, chilled in the refrigerator for at least an hour

¾ cup (1½ sticks) unsalted butter, softened

2 large eggs

1 cup sugar

1 teaspoon vanilla extract

1 cup cake flour, sifted

1 teaspoon baking powder

¼ teaspoon salt

½ cup milk

4 cups buttercream frosting, such as Vanilla Buttercream Frosting (page 50)

Sprinkles, to garnish (optional)

Adjust oven rack to the middle position and preheat oven to 350 degrees F. Line two standard-size muffin tins with cupcake papers.

Remove your chilled mini-cupcakes from the fridge. If they were made using paper liners, remove the liners. Set aside.

In a stand mixer fitted with the paddle attachment, combine the butter, eggs, sugar, and vanilla and beat on low speed until thick and lightened in color, about 5 minutes. Whisk together the flour, baking powder, and salt in a separate bowl. Alternately add the flour mixture and milk to the butter mixture in several additions, beating on medium speed after each addition until smooth.

Fill the cupcake papers no more than halfway full of batter. Place the mini-cupcakes directly into the center of each batter-filled cup. The volume of the mini-cupcakes should make the level of unbaked batter rise so that it is filling ⅔ of each cup. If not, add a small amount of extra batter to the cups.

Place pans in the oven with a baking sheet underneath to catch any drips. Bake until light golden brown, about 25 minutes. The frosting from the mini-cupcakes may have melted over the sides a bit, but you should still be able to see if the cake has browned. Don't panic if the melted frosting from the mini-cupcakes has made the top of your bigger cupcakes look ugly. They still taste good, and you'll be covering them with frosting, anyway.

Remove from the oven and let cool on wire racks. Once fully cooled, top the cupcakes with frosting. If desired, garnish with sprinkles.

Cupcakes Stuffed with Chocolate Chip Cookie Dough

Nobody's going to challenge the idea that cupcakes are delicious. But you know what? They're even better when stuffed with cookie dough. I learned this, of course, when I found myself with a boatload of extra rainbow chip cake mix and cookie dough from making a Cookie Cake Pie (page 73) and decided to make a batch of cupcakes with a dollop of dough dropped in each one.

CAKESPY NOTE: *Now, if you've never done it yourself, here's what you can expect.*

First, a heads-up: the cookie dough will sink—but this is OK, because as the cake bakes around and over the dough, each one develops an unexpected, gooey little sugar bomb inside. Since it will be gooey, the safest option might be to use an egg-free cookie dough.

Second, and perhaps more importantly: It will delight you and your friends to eat them.

24 SERVINGS

1 box rainbow chip cake mix (I like Funfetti)

About 1 cup chocolate chip cookie dough, homemade or store-bought

3 cups Chocolate Fudge Buttercream Frosting (recipe follows)

Line a standard cupcake pan with paper liners. Prepare the batter per instructions on the box. Fill the cups about two-thirds full, then give each one an added dose of awesome by dropping in a generous spoonful of cookie dough.

Bake as directed on your cake mix box, but keep in mind that the addition of the cookie dough may add 5 minutes or so to your bake time. Insert a cake tester or toothpick. Since the gooey texture of the cookie dough and chocolate may prevent the tester from coming out clean, instead look for a lack of crumbs

FACT: cookie dough makes everything better.

clinging to your cake tester to test doneness. Remove from the oven and let cool on wire racks.

Spread the frosting on the cooled cupcakes.

CHOCOLATE FUDGE BUTTERCREAM FROSTING

3 CUPS

½ cup (1 stick) butter, softened

¼ cup vegetable shortening

⅓ cup unsweetened cocoa powder

2 cups confectioners' sugar

2 tablespoons milk, plus 2 more tablespoons as needed

1 cup hot fudge topping, at room temperature (often labeled as "hot fudge ice cream topping" in stores)

1 teaspoon vanilla extract

In the bowl of a stand mixer fitted with the paddle attachment, cream the butter with the shortening until very smooth, about 2 minutes on medium speed. Sift the cocoa powder with the confectioners' sugar and add to the creamed mixture. Mix, using the slowest speed, while adding 1 tablespoon of milk at a time to thin and smooth the mixture. You should not need to add more than ¼ cup of milk in total. Add the hot fudge topping and the vanilla. Blend until smooth and creamy.

Cupcakes Baked in Ice Cream Cones

Why in the world would you bake a cupcake in an ice cream cone? Well, aside from the obvious reason (it looks cool!), it also serves a purpose: this festive preparation method reduces messes, since the entire handheld package is eatable. No messy cupcake wrappers hanging around and being dropped on the floor like a banana-peel joke waiting to happen.

18 TO 24 CONECAKES

1 batch of your favorite cupcake batter, homemade or from a cake mix

18 to 24 flat-bottom ice cream cones

3 to 4 cups buttercream frosting, such as Vanilla Buttercream Frosting (page 50), or Cocoa Buttercream Frosting (page 76)

Preheat the oven and prepare the cake batter as specified in your recipe.

Place the ice cream cones in a muffin tin, one cone per cup. To keep the filled cones from tipping, scrunch a piece of foil in the bottom of each cup and wedge the cone inside it.

Using an ice cream scoop or large spoon, drop rounded spoonfuls of batter into each cone. They should be about two-thirds full (you may end up filling fewer than 24 cones).

Very gently, place the pan into the oven (these cones want to fall, trust me). Bake for 15 to 20 minutes or until a toothpick inserted into the center of the cakes comes out clean (cones may tilt).

Cool completely, about 30 minutes. Generously top with frosting and decorate as desired.

Whoopie Pie Cupcakes

Not long ago, I attended a festival called CupcakeCamp in Seattle, where hundreds of cupcake enthusiasts, both professional and amateur, came together to share (and eat) cupcakes. But one submission made my eyes go wider than any other: whoopie pie cupcakes, the invention of none other than Audrey McManus, manager of Seattle's women-run adult store, Babeland (see how I am, very maturely, avoiding "making whoopie" jokes here?). Here it was: cold, hard proof that both cupcakes and whoopie pies are improved when combined. Yes! Needless to say it was love at first bite, and I rushed home to recreate the magic in my own kitchen. I divided up a batch of whoopie pie batter between cupcake liners and the traditional cookie form, and then brought these two worlds together with a generous dab of frosting.

The conclusion? Whoopie pies and cupcakes are definitely better together.

12 SERVINGS

For the cakes and cookie tops:

2¼ cups all-purpose flour

1¼ cups sugar

½ cup unsweetened cocoa powder

1½ teaspoons baking soda

1 teaspoon salt

⅔ cup butter, softened

2 large eggs

2 teaspoons vanilla extract

1 cup whole milk or half-and-half

For the filling:

4 cups Vanilla Buttercream Frosting (page 50), or one 16-ounce jar marshmallow crème

Preheat the oven to 350 degrees F. Prepare two baking pans: one muffin tin lined with paper cups and one baking sheet, lined with parchment paper.

Sift together the flour, sugar, cocoa powder, baking soda, and salt. Set to the side.

In a stand mixer fitted with the paddle attachment, cream the butter, eggs, and vanilla on medium speed, pausing to scrape the bowl as needed, until light and incorporated (it will not get fluffy). Add the sifted dry ingredients in three additions, alternating with the milk, until you have a smooth, creamy batter. It will be slightly thinner than typical drop-cookie dough.

Using either a cookie scoop or a heaping tablespoon, form 12 rounds of cookie dough onto the baking sheet. Shape them lightly so that the mounds of dough are about two thirds the circumference of the cupcake cups (they will spread to match). Space the cookie dough mounds about 1½ inches apart.

Using the remaining dough, fill each cupcake paper two-thirds full (you should have enough to fill 12 cups).

Bake until lightly browned around the edges (these are a lighter chocolate color than some whoopie pies, so you will see light browning). For the cookie tops, this will be 8 to 10 minutes; for the cupcakes, 15 to 20 minutes. A toothpick inserted into the cupcakes should come out clean. You can bake both pans at the same time; simply remove the tops from the oven sooner, leaving the cupcakes to bake a bit longer. Let the cupcakes and cookie tops cool completely on wire racks.

Using a spoon or an offset spatula, place a dollop of frosting on top of each cupcake. Gently place one of the cookie tops onto the frosting and press down gently. Repeat with the remaining cakes.

Pies in the Sky

STUFF YOUR PIE-HOLE WITH THESE INSPIRED SWEET TREATS

Cookie Cake Pie

Brownie Pie

Doughnut Pies

Pie Fries

Ice Cream Pudding Pie

Magic Cookie Bar Pie

Pookie, a Cookie-Coated Pie

Cookie Cake Pie

Cookies, cakes, and pies are basically the holy trinity of baked goods. Each is wonderful in its own way. But what if—just what if—all of this awesomeness could be combined into one singular sensation? It's time to break out a seriously sweet triple play: the Cookie Cake Pie. This treat embraces the idea that if some is good, more is wonderful; it weighs an almost obscene amount and it packs a dazzlingly sugary punch. Excessive? Perhaps. But everyone who tried it all but licked the plate clean.

12 SERVINGS

1 batch (about 2 cups) of your favorite cookie dough, homemade or store-bought

1 unbaked 9-inch piecrust

½ batch of your favorite cake batter, homemade or from a mix

2 to 3 cups frosting or other topping, such as whipped cream

First, prepare the cookie dough. If you choose to use the kind that comes in a tube from the supermarket, I promise I will not judge you. Whichever you choose, be sure to bring the cookie dough to room temperature before assembling the pie, so that it will be easier to spread.

Place the pie dough in a 9-inch pie plate.

Place the cookie dough on top of the piecrust and, using your fingers or the back of a spoon, spread the dough so that it evenly coats the bottom of the crust. It should be about ½ to ¾ inch thick. You will probably have extra cookie dough; you can use this as you'd like (to stuff cupcakes, as on page 64; to stuff some cinnamon rolls, as on page 2; or to have a delicious cookie dough snack). Set your cookie dough–filled piecrust aside.

Preheat the oven to 350 degrees F.

Make the cake batter as specified in your recipe and then pour it directly on top of the cookie dough until the piecrust is about two-thirds filled (the cake will rise, so you want to leave room for it to do so). You will probably have leftover cake batter; you can use this along with your extra cookie dough to make cookie dough–filled cupcakes (page 64).

Place the filled pie plate on a baking sheet (to catch any drips). To ensure that the sides of the cake don't bake too fast, gently place a piece of aluminum foil along the perimeter of the pie, leaving the center exposed.

Put your weighty pie-monster in the preheated oven and bake for 30 minutes. At this point, take the pie out of the oven and remove the aluminum foil; return to the oven and bake for another 15 to 25 minutes, or until the top is domed and golden, and a cake tester comes out mostly clean. Since the types of dough and batter will vary depending on the choices you've made, you might want to start checking for doneness after the initial 30 minutes.

Let cool. If the pretty domed top of your pie collapses, don't despair; it is just more of a void to fill with frosting. Frost generously with your choice of topping. Garnish as desired. I'd like to tell you how long this confection will keep, but mine has never lasted more than a day.

Brownie Pie

Brownies. Pie. Relegated to separate quadrants of the baked goods world, always on separate shelves in bakery cases. But why, when they're so much better together? In the spirit of sweet unity, I'd like to present the Brownie Pie. Comprised of a chocolate cookie crust; rich, fudgy brownie filling; and a topping of copious amounts of luxuriant cocoa buttercream frosting and a festive array of malt balls, this baby weighs about the same as (if not more than) a newborn. Of course, it's a good thing it's not actually a baby—otherwise you might be coming closer to understanding why some species eat their young.

CAKESPY NOTE: *Make sure that the frosting is of an easily spreadable consistency. Because brownies have a flaky texture on top, you want to be sure that the frosting spreads with ease and won't bring up too many of the crumbs (that just looks messy!).*

12 SERVINGS

One 9-inch chocolate cookie piecrust

1 batch of your favorite brownie recipe, homemade or from a mix

4 cups Cocoa Buttercream Frosting (recipe follows)

Malted milk balls or chocolate candies, to garnish (optional)

Prepare the piecrust: either bake it yourself or remove the plastic from your store-bought version.

Prepare the brownie batter according to the directions in your recipe. But at the point where you would normally put the batter in a pan, instead pour it into the piecrust. Fill the piecrust about two-thirds full, spreading the batter to the edges. You might have extra brownie batter.

Place the pie on top of a baking sheet (just in case of overflow) at the temperature specified in your recipe; test the doneness by inserting a toothpick or skewer into the center and making sure it comes out mostly clean. Remove the brownie pie from the oven, and let it cool to room temperature on a wire rack.

Spread the frosting on top of the brownie pie, leaving a little bit of the brownie showing along the edges. If desired, garnish with malted milk balls or other chocolate candies.

COCOA BUTTERCREAM FROSTING

4 CUPS

1 cup (2 sticks) butter, softened

¼ cup unsweetened cocoa powder

3 tablespoons milk

1 teaspoon vanilla extract

4 to 6 cups confectioners' sugar, sifted

In a stand mixer fitted with a paddle attachment, cream the butter. With the machine set at its lowest speed, add the cocoa powder and mix well. Add the milk and vanilla and mix until incorporated. Slowly beat in the confectioners' sugar, starting with 4 cups and adding more until the frosting is easily spreadable, almost like the consistency of whipped butter.

Doughnut Pies

Doughnuts play nice, don't they? They're so open to collaboration. You can make doughnut-bread pudding. Doughnut Upside-Down Cake (page 47). Doughnut burgers. And now, Doughnut Pie. While these may look like everyday doughnuts, don't be fooled. They're in fact little morsels of piecrust with filling rolled inside of them and then fried. While they're certainly not health food, they certainly are delicious: crispy, not too sweet, easy to make, and completely open to flavor improvisations.

15 TO 20 DOUGHNUT PIES

1 unbaked 9-inch piecrust

1½ cups jam, preserves, or filling of your choice

1 large egg, well beaten

1 cup frosting, such as Vanilla Buttercream Frosting (page 50) or Chocolate Fudge Buttercream Frosting (page 65) (optional)

Sprinkles, to garnish (optional)

Roll out the piecrust, and then cut it into strips. The strips should be about 2½ inches wide, and anywhere from 4 to 6 inches long, depending on what size doughnut you'd like.

Spoon a small amount of filling lengthwise down the center of each strip. Be sure to leave a small gap of uncovered dough along the long, narrow edges, and at both the top and bottom of the piece of dough.

Whisk the egg in a small bowl with one tablespoon of water until smooth; using a small pastry brush, lightly brush one of the long, narrow edges of dough with your egg wash. Gently fold the unbrushed side of the crust over the filling lengthwise, pinching it lightly with fingers or the tines of a fork on top of the side brushed with the egg wash, so that you have a long, narrow "log" of filled piecrust with filling inside. Don't worry about the look of the "seam"—later on, frosting the tops of your doughnut pies will cover this up.

Form the log into a circle, pinching the ends together so that they slightly over-lap. You can brush the fastened ends with a little more egg wash to ensure that they stay together.

Set up a large skillet or frying pan with about 1 inch of vegetable or canola oil covering the bottom, and set to high heat. Monitor the temperature until the oil has reached 375 degrees F, and then gently place the doughnuts several at a time into the pan, frying each side about 1 to 2 minutes or until golden. Take care when flipping the doughnut pies, as they are fairly delicate (they become sturdier as they cool).

Using a slotted spoon, gently remove the doughnuts from the pan and place on paper towels to blot excess oil. I'm not going to lie: the doughnut pies, at this point, are not extremely attractive. Don't worry—this is why we garnish them to serve.

Serve with additional fruit pie filling, whipped cream, ice cream, or—for a more classic doughnut look—a thick smear of frosting with plenty of sprinkles.

Pie Fries

When it comes to pie, my mantra is "I must increase my crust." But even carbohydrate addicts find themselves with extra scraps of pie dough from time to time. And I now have the best solution for making use of them: Pie Fries. I came across this idea from Seattle pie-baker Dani Cone (whom I suspect is a genius) and whose wonderful shop, High 5 Pie, offers some of the best pies in the country. The concept behind these pie fries is simple: just put your dough scraps on a baking sheet, slice them into French fry–size pieces, brush with butter, cinnamon, and sugar, and bake until crispy. Want extra "cute points"? Put 'em into pillow boxes (available at most craft supply stores) or paper cones and serve with jam for dipping.

2 TO 3 SERVINGS

Pie dough scraps leftover from preparing a 9-inch pie

Melted butter

Granulated sugar

Cinnamon, nutmeg, or other spices of your choice

Jam or preserves for dipping

Preheat the oven to 375 degrees F.

Collect your pie dough scraps. They may already be in slivers; if not, put them together into one clump, and roll the dough to about ⅛ inch thick. It's OK if the dough is not perfect looking when it's rolled out. Slice the dough into "fries" that are approximately the size of those you get in fast-food restaurants. Place the cut "fries" on a baking sheet lined with parchment paper. If the dough has gotten warm and hard to handle by this point, put it into the refrigerator until it firms up, about 20 minutes.

Using a pastry brush, brush the fries with a little (or a lot) of butter, and sprinkle with the sugar, cinnamon, and other spices. Bake for 10 minutes, or until golden brown and crispy around the edges.

If you're going for those extra cute points, cut pillow boxes in half for a sweet presentation. If desired, affix labels. If you're going for a *très chic* look, serve in paper cones, like they do in Belgium. Serve in the assembled cones or boxes with jam on the side for dipping.

PIE DOUGH COOKIES. Not into fries? It's OK. Go ahead and gather your pie dough scraps and roll them out, but instead of cutting into French fry shapes, use cookie cutters (bonus points if you use one shaped like a unicorn). Brush with butter, sugar, and spices as specified in the Pie Fries recipe, and bake until golden. Enjoy.

Pie Fries!

Ice Cream Pudding Pie

Topping the list of things I'll never do again? Preparing instant-pudding pie filling with cold milk. Why? Because as it turns out, it's far more delicious when you make it with melted ice cream. And when you go for chocolate on both counts (pudding and ice cream), you'll be rewarded with the most luxuriant chocolate cream pie filling you've ever tasted. The thick, velvety chocolate mixture falls somewhere between pudding pop and mousse in texture, and it's so deeply, darkly, completely chocolatey in flavor that you won't want the slice to end.

8 SERVINGS

1 unbaked 9-inch piecrust, or a graham cracker or cookie crust

1 large package (5.9 ounces) instant chocolate pudding

2 cups melted chocolate ice cream

Whipped cream for topping (optional)

Bake the piecrust according to your recipe or the package instructions and set it aside to cool.

Put the pudding mix and the melted ice cream in a large bowl and mix them by hand, using a whisk, until the pudding mix is completely dissolved. This may take several minutes. Spoon the mixture into your prepared piecrust; it will be rather thick. Using an offset spatula, smooth the filling so that it is evenly distributed.

Refrigerate the pie for 2 to 3 hours to let it set. If desired, top with a heap of whipped cream before serving.

Magic Cookie Bar Pie

Magic Cookie Bars are, as their name might imply, no ordinary treat. Starting with layer upon layer of unrelentingly rich, buttery graham cracker crumbs, toasted coconut, chocolate and butterscotch chips, and nuts, they get even better when they're smothered in rich sweetened condensed milk. With all that awesome, some might argue that a small serving is best. But I disagree, and to prove it, I've created those magical bars in pie form, which is naturally best served in thick, fat wedges. You're welcome.

CAKESPY NOTE: *The peanut butter is not traditional in this recipe, but it is, as my nephew would solemnly say, "very yummy." If you want to stay true to the original, you can use a cup of toasted and chopped pecans, walnuts, or peanuts instead.*

12 SERVINGS

For the crust:

¾ cup (1½ sticks) butter

1 cup sweetened shredded coconut, toasted

1¾ cups finely ground graham cracker crumbs

For the filling:

½ cup peanut butter, smooth or chunky

1 cup semisweet chocolate chips

¾ cup butterscotch chips

One 14-ounce can sweetened condensed milk

Preheat the oven to 300 degrees F. Butter a 9-inch pie plate.

Melt the butter in a medium saucepan pan over low heat; add the coconut and graham cracker crumbs and stir until the mixture is well combined. Let this mixture cool until it is still warm but not too hot to handle; using your hands, press the mixture into the bottom and up the sides of the pie plate.

Refrigerate the crust for 15 minutes, then bake it for 10 minutes, or until golden brown. If the crust slumps at all, just wait until it is not too hot to touch, then pat it back into place with your fingers. Let the crust cool at room temperature for at least 20 minutes.

Increase the oven temperature to 325 degrees F.

Place the peanut butter in teaspoon-size dollops, evenly distributed on top of the crust (think polka-dot pattern).

Scatter the chocolate chips and butterscotch chips on top of the peanut-buttered crust.

Pour the sweetened condensed milk in a slow, steady stream over the filling, then gently shake the pan to make sure the liquid has settled evenly.

Bake for 30 to 40 minutes, or until golden brown and bubbly.

Remove from the oven, transfer to a wire rack and let cool completely before serving.

Pookie, a Cookie-Coated Pie

Pie and cookies are both very enjoyable on their own. But together? Far more awesome. In this recipe, an already-good pie gets a delicious upgrade by way of an allover cookie coating. Like a buttery blanket, the cookie coating is absolutely ravishing with the contrasting texture but equally rich taste of the piecrust. Put on your fat pants and enjoy.

10 SERVINGS

1 cup (2 sticks) butter, softened

1 cup packed brown sugar

½ cup granulated sugar

2 large eggs

1½ teaspoons vanilla extract

3 cups all-purpose flour, plus extra for handling dough

½ teaspoon salt

1 bag (11 ounces) butterscotch chips

One double-crusted 8-inch apple pie, homemade or purchased; if homemade, bake in a tin pie plate for easy removal

Preheat the oven to 350 degrees F.

Butter a 10-inch pie plate and line it with two crisscrossed strips of parchment paper for easy removal later. Set aside.

In the bowl of an electric mixer fitted with the paddle attachment, cream the butter, brown sugar, and granulated sugar on medium speed until light and fluffy. Add the eggs one at a time, beating well and scraping down the sides of the bowl after each addition. Add the vanilla.

Sift the flour and salt into a separate small bowl. Add the dry ingredients to the wet mixture, mixing until just combined, pausing to scrape down the sides of the bowl as needed. Using a spatula or large spoon, fold in the butterscotch chips.

Using floured hands, press a layer of cookie dough into the bottom and up the sides of the pie plate. Remove the whole apple pie from its tin (if necessary) and place it on top of the cookie dough. To cover the top of the pie, form a large (baseball-size) ball of cookie dough, and flatten with your hands. Place this on top of the exposed pie top and very gently pat it down; use the remaining cookie dough to fill in any gaps on the top or sides, so that the pie is completely covered in cookie dough on all sides. If you have extra dough, save it to bake as cookies or to fill cupcakes (page 64).

Bake for 40 to 50 minutes, or until the pookie is crispy on the edges and the surface of the cookie dough takes on a dull finish.

Let cool; if desired, serve à la mode.

Sweet Nothings

CANDY, CONFECTIONS, AND TREATS ON A STICK THAT ARE A MOUTHFUL OF FUN

Velveeta Fudge

Candy Salad

Inside-Out Peanut Butter Cups

Deep-Fried Cupcakes on a Stick

Pie Pops

Kebabka

Velveeta Fudge

Contrary to popular belief, Velveeta's main contribution to society isn't as a topping for cheap nachos; turns out, it's also an important component of a Deep South regional variety of fudge. Hey, I was skeptical when I discovered it, too, but after one bite I was converted. This fudge is incredibly rich, with a creaminess and subtle savory undertone from the Velveeta. Basically, everyone loves it until they hear what the key ingredient is—so I say, unless there are dietary concerns, don't tell 'em what won't hurt 'em.

36 SMALL PIECES

1 cup (2 sticks) butter, softened

8 ounces pasteurized processed cheese (such as Velveeta), cubed

2 teaspoons vanilla extract

2 cups coarsely chopped pecans or walnuts

8 cups confectioners' sugar

½ cup unsweetened cocoa powder

Lightly spray a 9-inch square baking pan with nonstick spray, or grease with butter.

In a saucepan over medium heat, melt the butter and cheese, stirring constantly until smooth. Remove from the heat and add the vanilla and nuts.

In a separate large bowl, sift together the sugar and cocoa. Pour the cheese mixture into the cocoa mixture and stir until completely mixed. The candy will be very stiff.

Using your hands, a rubber spatula, or the back of a large spoon, transfer the candy from the bowl to the pan, pressing evenly and firmly. Because the butter and processed cheese sometimes form excess oil as they set in the pan, if needed, pat the top of the candy with a paper towel to remove the excess. Grossed out? Just power through it—you will be rewarded in the end. Place pan in the refrigerator and chill until candy is firm.

To serve, cut the fudge into squares. Or slabs. Your call.

Candy Salad

I am not going to lie to you: this salad is not health food. But you know what? It looks like health food when you squint really hard at it, and it tastes a lot better. In my opinion, it totally fulfills your New Year's resolutions: after all (and I know that a dietitian, somewhere, is shedding more than a single tear over me saying this), you are eating your greens.

CAKESPY NOTE: *What on earth is a "candy melt wafer"? Well. These little wafers are sort of like an easy-melt version of white chocolate; they're available in a variety of different colors and flavors, and work beautifully for molded candies and confections. My favorite type, available in all of the colors of the rainbow, goes by the brand name Merckens.*

2 SERVINGS

¾ cup green candy melt wafers

4 to 5 pieces of marzipan, colored red with food coloring and formed into "tomato" shaped rounds

1 slice pound cake, cut into ½-inch cubes and fried in butter (see Cadbury Creme Eggs Benedict, page 15)

Lay out a 14-inch-long piece of plastic wrap on the countertop. In a medium microwave-safe bowl (or in the top of a double boiler), melt the candy melts, stirring occasionally until smooth.

Let the candy cool slightly, but do not let it begin to harden.

Pour the candy onto one side of the plastic wrap. Fold the other half of the plastic wrap over the still-warm candy. Gently smooth down with your hands to your desired thickness (no thinner than ⅛ inch thick, or it will break!).

Wrinkle the still-warm candy gently with your fingers to mimic the little wrinkles and ripples of lettuce leaves. Let the candy cool in the plastic wrap for 20 to 30 minutes, or until it is brittle. Gently remove the plastic wrap. Some small

pieces may break along the edges, but don't worry. Lettuce is usually irregularly shaped, anyway!

Using a knife or your fingers, break the candy into chunks; arrange it artfully on a small plate to resemble a salad. Top with your marzipan "tomato slices" and fried "croutons" of pound cake.

Inside-Out Peanut Butter Cups

Chocolate peanut butter cups are undoubtedly one of the finer things in life. But I have my reservations about their basic construction: the chocolate gets your hands messy and there never seems to be enough peanut butter. The happy solution? Turn them inside out, so that the shell is made of peanut butter, and the insides are filled with chocolate. While the crumbly nature of the crust doesn't make them much neater to eat, tastewise it's a whole new ball game. It's like the fudgy center is getting a big peanut butter bear hug from the cookie coating.

11 LARGE PEANUT BUTTER CUPS

For the peanut butter shells:

¼ cup (½ stick) butter, softened

¼ cup plus 2 tablespoons packed light brown sugar

2½ tablespoons peanut butter (creamy works best)

¼ teaspoon vanilla extract

1 cup all-purpose flour

For the filling:

2 tablespoons whole milk

1 tablespoon peanut butter (creamy works best)

1 tablespoon unsweetened cocoa powder

1 tablespoon butter, softened

½ teaspoon vanilla extract

Preheat the oven to 350 degrees F. Place 12 regular-size paper cupcake liners in a muffin tin.

In a mixing bowl, using a wooden spoon or by hand, cream the butter, brown sugar, peanut butter, and vanilla until light and fluffy. Gradually add the flour until combined; the mixture should be fairly crumbly.

In 11 of the cupcake liners, press about 2 tablespoons of the peanut butter mixture into the bottom half of the cupcake cups, making sure to press the mixture firmly into the bottom and up the sides so that it forms a shallow cup shape (the mixture will only come about halfway up the sides of the cups).

In the one remaining cupcake liner, lightly press the rest of the peanut butter cookie mixture into the cup (this will be crumbled on the top of the rest of the cups later); it should nearly fill the last cup. If you have any remaining cookie mixture, use it to fill in any gaps in the 11 firmly packed cups.

Bake for 12 to 15 minutes, or until lightly browned and set. Let cool for 10 minutes.

While the peanut butter shells bake, make the filling. Combine all of the ingredients in a small saucepan on low heat, stirring occasionally, until combined and creamy. Pour a small amount of the chocolate mixture (about ½ tablespoon) into the center of each of the peanut butter cups (it is ok if they are still warm).

Using the crumble mixture baked in the one full cup, crumble a small amount (about ½ tablespoon) on top of each chocolate-topped cup; this should mostly cover the chocolate.

Refrigerate for 1 hour, or until the filling has set.

Deep-Fried Cupcakes on a Stick

First things first. The title of this recipe has probably brought up a serious question, and I'd like to answer it straightaway. The answer is yes, I am trying to kill you, Paula Deen–style. These deep-fried cupcakes on sticks probably won't make it any easier to stick to your New Year's resolution plan, but they're delicious. The thick batter seals moisture into the cake, and adds a glorious carbohydrate punch that makes them absolutely tantalizing. The taste is like the intersection of childhood nostalgia and greasy fair food.

CAKESPY NOTE: *You can also put other cakes and candies on a stick, including Twinkies and snack cakes of all sorts, or even leftover Halloween candy!*

12 SERVINGS

12 frosted mini cupcakes, wrappers removed

6 to 8 cups vegetable oil for frying

1½ cups all-purpose flour, divided

1 teaspoon baking soda

½ teaspoon salt

1 cup milk

1 tablespoon white vinegar

1 tablespoon vegetable oil

At least 2 hours before you begin frying, freeze the cupcakes. First, place them on a plate or baking sheet. Insert one popsicle stick into the center of each cupcake bottom and freeze for at least 2 hours, until they are completely frozen.

When you're ready to proceed, start heating the oil for frying. Pour the vegetable oil into a large, heavy-bottomed saucepan until it is 3 inches deep (the amount of oil you use will depend on the size of your saucepan). Turn the heat to medium-high and attach a deep-fry thermometer to the side of the pan. Heat until the oil reaches 375 degrees F.

While you're waiting for the oil to heat up, prepare the batter and set up your frying station. Place ½ cup of the flour in a bowl and set aside. Place the remaining 1 cup of flour in a small bowl and mix with the baking soda and salt; add the milk, vinegar, and oil, then whisk until you have a relatively lump-free, thick batter.

Remove the frozen cupcakes from the freezer. It's go time.

Dredge each cupcake in flour, and then in batter, covering it completely. Holding the end of the stick, quickly and carefully lower the battered cupcake into the heated oil. Be very careful not to drop it or cause oil to splash (in fact, I'd recommend that you wear a glove for safety). Once the batter has reached an appealing golden hue, after 30 seconds or so, lift the cupcake from the hot oil and place it on a plate lined with several paper towels. Repeat the battering and frying process with the remaining cupcakes. Be sure to monitor the temperature of the oil and adjust the heat up or down accordingly, as the frosting on the cupcakes will melt if the oil is too hot, and it will take too long to fry and become greasy if the heat is too low.

Let the cupcakes cool slightly; they are best served warm and crisp.

Pie Pops

Riddle me this: what doesn't taste better on a stick? While you ponder that epic question, let me introduce you to a pint-size pop of flavor, far more satisfying than any lollipop, and guaranteed to delight your dining companions after (or, for that matter, before or in between) any meal: Pie Pops. These pops are ideal for crust lovers, providing a high crust-to-filling ratio.

24 PIE POPS

Double crust for a 9-inch pie, unbaked

1 cup pie filling of your choice (use pie fillings that would be baked in an unbaked pie shell—apple pie, pumpkin pie, chess pies, etc.); or, simply use jam or preserves

1 large egg, well beaten

Preheat the oven to 400 degrees F.

On a floured surface, roll the first of your two crusts to a 10-inch diameter (as if you were rolling it out for a 9-inch pie). Lightly flour the top of the rolled crust and, using a cookie cutter, biscuit cutter, or even an overturned drinking glass, cut out as many circles or rounds as you can. The diameter of your cutter should be about 2 inches. Gather the scraps of dough and roll them out to get a few more cutouts. Repeat with the second piecrust.

Place half of the cutouts onto two baking sheets, 12 per sheet, in two rows of six on each sheet. Leave plenty of space between the rows to allow room for the lollipop sticks. Press a lollipop stick on top of each cutout, making sure that the stick hits three-forths of the way up the cutout.

Place the remaining half of the cutouts in the refrigerator while you complete the next steps, so that they will remain firm and easy to handle when you are ready to use them.

Place a small spoonful (about 1 teaspoon) of pie filling in the center of each cutout, covering the lollipop stick and leaving about one forth inch around the outside edge of each circle.

Whisk the egg in a small bowl with one tablespoon of water until smooth; using a small pastry brush, lightly brush the perimeter of each dough round with the egg wash (this will help the top piece adhere to the bottom).

Gently place a second cutout on top of the bottom pieces. Use the tines of a fork to press all around the sides of each circle. This will ensure that the pie pops are sealed and that the filling will not leak out.

If a small amount of filling comes out while you are doing this, it's OK. Last, using the fork, poke a few holes into the top of each pie pop to allow steam to escape while baking.

For a glossy golden finish, brush the tops of the pie pops lightly with the egg wash.

Place the pie pops in the oven. Bake for 8 to 12 minutes, or until golden around the edges.

Kebabka

Sometimes, foods on a stick are too small to be truly satisfying. Happily, there is a food on a stick that will stick with you: delicious chunks of chocolate babka (a rich, yeast-risen coffee cake made in a variety of flavors, although we all know chocolate is best), speared kebab-style on a skewer—or, as I like to call it, kebabka. Now, kebabka is not necessarily a cute food. It's not delicate, and it's not dainty. But it is rich, choco-latey, carbohydratey, and delicious—and when enjoyed several chunks at a time eaten directly off of a stick, it will not leave you hungry.

15 SERVINGS

For the babka:

½ cup (1 stick) butter, softened

½ cup sugar

4 large eggs, separated

1 package (2½ teaspoons) active dry yeast

¼ cup lukewarm water

1 cup whole milk

1 teaspoon vanilla extract

1 teaspoon salt

2 cups all-purpose flour

For the filling:

½ cup (1 stick) butter

One 3.5-ounce bar dark or semisweet chocolate

2 tablespoons whipping cream

In a stand mixer fitted with the paddle attachment, cream the butter and sugar until smooth. In a medium-size bowl, stir the egg yolks until creamy (save some of the egg whites to use later for an egg wash). Set aside.

Mix the yeast in warm water with a large pinch of sugar. After several minutes, stir to make sure the yeast is dissolved, and then add it to the egg yolks, along with the milk, vanilla, and salt. Add the yeast mixture to the butter and sugar and mix briefly. Scrape down the sides of the bowl. Slowly add the flour and mix until a smooth, soft dough forms.

Turn the dough out onto a floured work surface and knead it until it is no longer sticky, dusting the dough and the board with flour as needed. Put the dough into a bowl, cover with plastic wrap, and allow it to rise in a warm place until it doubles in size, about 1 hour.

Meanwhile, prepare the filling: place the butter, chocolate, and whipping cream in a medium saucepan or double boiler over low heat and stir until melted and smooth. Remove from the heat and set to the side.

Turn the dough out onto a floured work surface and roll it out into a large rectangle about 9 by 12 inches. Cut it horizontally into 15 strips using a sharp knife or a pizza cutter.

Before proceeding, prepare two muffin tins, lining one with 8 paper cup liners, and the second with the remaining liners (dividing them this way rather than completely filling one tin will help them bake more evenly).

Stretch out one of the strips of dough and spoon about 1 tablespoon of chocolate filling on top. Roll it like you would a cinnamon roll (this will be a little messy) and set it into a cupcake cup. Repeat with the remaining strips of dough. They should take up about two thirds of the volume of the cupcake cups. Reserve any extra chocolate filling; you can use this later to drizzle on top of the cakes before baking.

Cover the pans loosely with plastic wrap and let rise again until they have puffed up over the top of the paper liners, about an hour.

Preheat the oven to 350 degrees F.

Use the leftover egg whites to lightly brush on top of each little loaf to ensure a pleasing golden tone.

At this point, drizzle any of the leftover chocolate topping over the risen dough mounds.

Bake for 25 to 30 minutes, or until golden and crispy on top. Let cool completely.

Cut each babka into either halves or fourths; spear one cut-up babka on each skewer, and then enjoy some awesome food on a stick. If desired, serve the kebabs with lightly sweetened whipped cream on the side for dipping.

The Big Chill

COLD TREATS THAT WILL MELT IN YOUR MOUTH

Red Velvet Cake Shake

Super-Salty Chocolate
Ice Cream

Toaster Pastry Ice Cream
Sandwiches

Two-Tone Pudding Pops

Banana Peanut Butter
Cookie Pudding

Dessert Tacos

Red Velvet Cake Shake

There's a reason why you've never tried a Red Velvet Cake Shake. That reason, of course, is that the recipe relies on you having an extra slice of red velvet cake lying around—and as anyone knows, this is a highly unlikely occurrence. However, after one fateful weekend of serious red cake overindulgence (don't ask), I found myself in this unusual situation. Unable to face another forkful, a beautiful phrase came to mind: Red Velvet Cake Shake. Could it possibly be as good as it sounded? Oh, yes. This shake has it all: tangy cream cheese frosting; rich, moist cake; and sweet, creamy ice cream—all mixed into one pretty, pink, pourable form.

CAKESPY NOTE: *Low-fat tip! If your instinct is to cry "too much!" I do have a suggestion: call it a smoothie. Don't you feel healthier already?*

1 SERVING

1 slice red velvet cake

2 very large scoops of ice cream (good flavor choices might be vanilla, caramel swirl, or strawberry)

½ to ¾ cup milk

Put all of the ingredients into a blender. Blend until the shake has reached your desired consistency—less if you like little bits of cake in your shake, longer if you like a smoother texture. Add more ice cream for a thicker shake or more milk for a thinner one.

INSTEAD OF A RED VELVET SLICE, see what other sweet treats can be stuffed in a shake. Some of my favorites? A slice of pie and a slice of cake (making for the "Pake Shake"), a Cupcake Milkshake, Pumpkin Pie Shake (in the unlikely event that you have leftover pie at Thanksgiving), or a Crumb Cake Shake.

Super-Salty Chocolate Ice Cream

Chocolate and salt: they just work better together. Cases in point: the killer combos of french fries with chocolate shakes, and chocolate-covered pretzels. But for an easy frozen fix for your sweet and salty pleasure, how about chocolate ice cream all mixed up with the salty treat of your choice? True, this may be a slightly trashy dessert, but it's also compulsively eatable and extremely addictive.

2 SERVINGS

4 large scoops chocolate ice cream, softened

2 slices bacon, cooked until very crisp, crumbled into small pieces, or 1 large handful crumbled potato chips

2 heaping spoonfuls peanut butter, melted in the microwave

¼ cup milk or heavy cream

Put all of the ingredients into a blender and mix until just combined. Transfer to a bowl and freeze until you're ready to serve, then scoop the ice cream into individual bowls.

Toaster Pastry Ice Cream Sandwiches

Did you know that the ice cream sandwich was invented in the early 1900s as a sanitary solution for serving ice cream on hot summer days? Well, times have changed—society and freezers have both evolved, and now, instead of sandwiching our ice cream between cookie wafers, we can serve it between layers of another modern marvel, the prebaked toaster pastry. While I favor the combo of frosted strawberry Pop-Tarts with strawberry ice cream, the flavor combinations are virtually endless.

4 SERVINGS

4 toaster pastries, homemade (page 5) or store-bought

4 large scoops ice cream, softened

Multi-colored pastel sprinkles, to garnish (optional)

Cut each toaster pastry in half, horizontally, so that you have two smaller rectangles.

Place a generous spoonful of ice cream on the insides of four pastry halves. Top them with the remaining pastry pieces, frosted side up. Lightly press together, then gently smooth the ice cream on the sides for an even, finished look.

Place the sprinkles in a shallow dish. Roll the edges of each sandwich in sprinkles. Wrap individually in waxed paper or plastic wrap; freeze for about 2 hours, or until firm.

Two-Tone Pudding Pops

Pudding pops are the frozen equivalent of "shake and bake"—basically, all you do is mix and freeze. However, with a modicum of effort, you can create two-toned treats that will make you seem like a true kitchen whiz kid.

12 SERVINGS

2 packages (3.4 ounces each) instant pudding, in different but complementary flavors

2 cups cold half-and-half, divided

2 cups cold milk, divided

You'll need 12 small paper "dixie" cups (3 ounces each) and 12 popsicle sticks. Have them close by while you make the puddings.

Combine one of the packages of instant pudding powder with 1 cup of the half-and-half and 1 cup of the milk, whisking until smooth. Pour the mixture into the cups; fill them about halfway full.

Repeat these steps in a separate bowl with the second flavor. Pour this mixture on top of the other pudding and fill the cups almost to the top. Insert the sticks; the bottom pudding should be set enough so that the sticks remain upright.

Freeze for 4 to 5 hours. Peel off the cups before serving.

Banana Peanut Butter Cookie Pudding

Banana Nilla Wafer Pudding is one of the creamiest, dreamiest desserts out there. Elvis ate it every night (it's rumored he would mash up his various prescription pills on top—talk about sweet dreams), and at New York City's famous Magnolia Bakery, it's the number-two seller (after their famous cupcakes). But you know what? I think it's even better when you replace the Nilla Wafers with peanut butter cookies, which offer a rich, salty undertone to the creamy pudding.

8 SERVINGS

One 14-ounce can sweetened condensed milk

1 cup ice-cold water

1 package (3.4 ounces) instant vanilla or French vanilla pudding

2 cups heavy whipping cream

3 cups coarsely crumbled peanut butter cookies

4 large or 5 small bananas, very ripe, sliced into coins

Extra peanut butter cookie halves, and/or whipped cream, for garnish

In a medium bowl, combine the sweetened condensed milk with the water, mixing with a wooden spoon until smooth. Add the instant pudding and mix vigorously until combined; the mixture will be very thick. Whip the cream to soft peaks, then gently fold it into the pudding mixture, stirring until creamy and uniformly colored.

To assemble the dessert, start with a deep-dish pie pan or casserole dish. On the bottom of the dish, make a checkerboard-type pattern using the cookie crumbs and banana slices. On top of this, spread a thick layer of pudding.

Repeat these steps, layering the remaining cookie crumbs and banana slices with the pudding once or twice more (this may vary due to the size of your chosen dish). Finish with pudding on top (otherwise the banana slices will turn brown). Refrigerate the dessert for at least 4 hours before serving so that the flavors and textures meld.

When ready to serve, make each portion pretty by serving in individual parfait glasses and garnishing with cookie wedges and/or whipped cream.

Dessert Tacos

Sometimes when you're at a gas station or convenience store, you'll come across a magical sight: in the frozen foods case, there will be something called the Choco Taco, a masterpiece of frozen food. Well, here they are, amigos, re-created for you and easily personalized to suit your unique dessert taco tastes.

8 SERVINGS

For the shells:

2 large eggs

½ cup sugar

¼ cup (½ stick) butter, melted

2 tablespoons heavy cream

½ teaspoon vanilla extract

⅓ cup all-purpose flour, sifted

¼ teaspoon salt

½ cup vegetable oil, for frying

1 package (12 ounces) chocolate chips

1 tablespoon shortening

For the filling:

About 4 cups chilled custard, pudding, or softened ice cream

Sprinkles, nuts, or chocolate chips, to garnish

Whisk together the eggs and sugar in a large bowl until frothy. Whisk in the melted butter, cream, and vanilla. Gradually add the flour and salt and whisk until smooth. The batter should be pourable, like pancake batter; stir in more cream to thin, if needed.

Heat a small nonstick skillet or griddle over medium heat. Pour a small amount of vegetable oil in the pan (enough to lightly coat it). Pour about ¼ cup of the batter onto the skillet; rotate the skillet to spread the batter into a thin circle

about 5 inches in diameter. When the underside is golden brown, flip it over and cook until golden on the other side. Remove the "taco shell" from the pan and, while it is still hot, drape it over the fat handle of a wooden spoon to form the shape of a hard taco shell. Once it is firm, insert a toothpick broken in half in the center, so that it retains its shape. Once it has cooled enough to hold its shape, place it on a wire rack to cool and harden completely. Repeat with the remaining batter. You should have about 8 shells. If they crack, don't panic, you may be able to "glue" them together with the chocolate coating. Regardless, they will still taste good.

Melt the chocolate chips and shortening in the top of a double boiler. Using a pastry brush, gently coat the inside of each shell with the chocolate mixture. Set them back on the wire rack or on waxed paper to cool.

In about 1 hour, or when the chocolate has completely hardened, spoon in your desired chilly filling—be it cannoli filling, pudding, ice cream, or (my favorite) frozen custard. Garnish with nuts, sprinkles, or more chocolate chips. Serve immediately, or wrap individually and keep in the freezer until ready to serve.

Seasonal Sweets

SWEET TREATS WITH HOLIDAYS IN MIND

NEW YEAR'S EVE/DAY
Mimosa Brownies

VALENTINE'S DAY
Homemade
Conversation Hearts

ST. PATRICK'S DAY
Leprechaun Shake

EASTER
Peeps S'mores

MOTHER'S DAY
Battenberg Cake

FATHER'S DAY
Sweet and Salty Brownies

4TH OF JULY
Pop Rocks Cookies

LABOR DAY
Cakes Grilled in Orange Shells

HALLOWEEN
Homemade Candy Corn

THANKSGIVING
Leftover Cranberry Sauce
Bar Cookies

HANUKKAH
Marshmallow Dreidels

CHRISTMAS
Ginger-Bread Pudding

NEW YEAR'S EVE/DAY
Mimosa Brownies

Happy New Year! Now, before you go and do anything silly, like start dieting, why not have one final hurrah with some Mimosa Brownies? Giving your brownies a champagne-and-orange juice makeover yields a festive treat that is equally delicious at a New Year's Eve party or on the morning after, for brunch.

CAKESPY NOTE: *You may notice that the amount of champagne used for this recipe is quite small; this will leave you plenty of bubbly to make actual mimosas to accompany the brownies. As for the use of orange juice concentrate versus orange juice: I find that it offers an essential bright orange flavor that elevates the chocolate to just the right level.*

24 SERVINGS

For the brownies:
1 batch of your favorite brownie recipe, homemade or from a mix

1 tablespoon orange juice concentrate, thawed

1 tablespoon champagne or sparkling wine

For the glaze:

½ cup champagne or sparkling wine

1 tablespoon orange juice concentrate, thawed

1½ to 2 cups confectioners' sugar, sifted

Prepare the brownies as specified in your recipe for an 8-by-8-inch pan, adding the orange juice concentrate and champagne last, and mixing only until incorporated. Bake as specified in the recipe.

Once the brownies have baked and cooled, prepare the glaze. In a medium bowl, mix the champagne, orange juice concentrate, and confectioners' sugar until combined. The mixture should be pourable but not too thin.

Slice the brownies and top each one with a spoonful of glaze right before serving, preferably alongside a big ol' glass of the remaining bubbly.

VALENTINE'S DAY
Homemade Conversation Hearts

Are you sending the wrong message with your conversation hearts? Do you really want, for instance, to say "text me" to someone from whom you'd rather not receive digital missives, or to downplay your serious crush by leaving it at "U R Special"? No, tell them how you really feel by making your own personalized homemade conversation hearts. They're surprisingly easy to make, and you have complete freedom to set the tone you want—whether it's sweet, snarky, or confessional.

CAKESPY NOTE: *It's essential that you plan ahead if you're going to deliver your Hearts on time. While these candies don't take long to make, they do require at least 24 hours to dry before you can write on them. If you rush this process, the ink will bleed.*

ABOUT 100 SMALL OR 70 LARGE CONVERSATION HEARTS

One ¼-ounce packet (2 teaspoons) unflavored gelatin

½ cup water

2 teaspoons light corn syrup

4 cups confectioners' sugar

Assorted food colors

Assorted flavoring extracts, such as almond, vanilla, mint, orange

Food coloring markers, such as Gourmet Writer Food Pens

Place the gelatin, water, and corn syrup in a small microwave-safe bowl. Stir until the gelatin is well distributed. Microwave the mixture for 30 seconds and stir again, making sure the gelatin has dissolved.

Pour the gelatin mixture into the bowl of a large stand mixer fitted with the paddle attachment. Alternately, if you are using a hand mixer, pour it into a large bowl. Add 1 cup of powdered sugar and mix at low speed until the mixture is smooth. Add another cup of sugar, again mixing on low speed until it liquefies. Continue to add powdered sugar, one cup at a time, until the full two pounds of powdered sugar has been added. Periodically stop the mixer and scrape down the bottom and sides of the bowl. The candy will progress from a thin, watery liquid to a very stiff dough.

Dust your countertop (or a large cutting board) with confectioners' sugar and scrape the candy out onto the work surface; it will be very sticky. Generously dust the top of the ball of candy with powdered sugar and knead the candy like bread dough: fold the ball of dough over onto itself, then use the heel of your hand to push it forward and down. Give the candy a quarter-turn and repeat the process, dusting it with more powdered sugar as often as necessary to prevent it from sticking. Knead until the candy is satiny and no longer sticky.

Decide how many colors/flavors of conversation hearts you want to make, and divide the candy dough into that many portions. Flatten each portion into a palm-size disc. Add a few drops of food coloring and flavoring extract to the center of the disc and fold it over on itself. (It's a good idea to wear disposable plastic gloves during this step to keep your hands free of colors and odors.) Knead the dough ball, just as you did before, until the color is evenly dispersed throughout the candy and all streaks have disappeared. Repeat this process with the remaining candy balls and colors/flavors.

Dust the work surface and a rolling pin with confectioners' sugar, and roll out one of the candy balls to your desired thickness. [Small store-bought conversation hearts are about ¼-inch thick. I find that this thickness works well for small hearts (under 1 inch in diameter), but it makes larger heart sizes rather difficult to eat. However, the thickness is entirely a matter of personal preference.]

Use heart-shaped cutters to cut the rolled candy. The size of the cutouts is up to you: smaller hearts look more realistic, but larger hearts are easier to write messages on. Transfer the hearts to a baking sheet lined with parchment paper. Reroll the scraps if you'd like to cut out more candy. Repeat with the remaining candy balls.

Allow your hearts to air-dry for at least 24 hours before you write on them. This step is very important, because any extra moisture in the hearts will cause the ink to run and look blurry.

When the candies are thoroughly dry, use the food writing markers to write messages or draw designs on the hearts. Store your conversation hearts in an airtight container at room temperature.

Leprechaun Shake

There is a shake, a magical shake, that beckons from a certain fast-food establishment known for its gilded arches. If you've found yourself curious, here's a way to make something just as satisfyingly unhealthy at home. So bad it's good, in a rot-your-teeth-out sort of way.

1 SERVING

2 large scoops green mint chocolate chip ice cream

¼ cup milk or heavy cream

Several drops green food coloring (optional)

Dash of crème de menthe (optional)

A healthy handful of shamrock-shaped sprinkles (optional, but so much more fun)

Place all of the ingredients except for the sprinkles in a blender. Blend until smooth. Add more ice cream for a thicker shake, more milk for a thinner one. Pour into a large glass and stir in the shamrock sprinkles.

EASTER
Peeps S'mores

Everyone loves putting Peeps in the microwave for entertainment (right?). So why not end up with something extra delicious for all that time and energy? In this recipe, s'mores get a visit from the Easter bunny when you substitute a pink rabbit peep for the usual marshmallow. As an unexpected bonus, the sugar coating on the peep lends a wonderfully satisfying, slightly crunchy texture to the already-pretty-wonderful classic s'more.

1 SERVING

1 graham cracker, broken in half to form two squares

2 rectangles from a regular-size Hershey's milk chocolate bar

1 bunny-shaped Peep

Place the chocolate rectangles on top of one cracker; put the Peep on top of that. Top the marshmallow with the remaining graham cracker.

Microwave on high for 10 to 15 seconds, or until the Peep has swelled and bubbled. The top half of the sandwich will likely fall off. That's OK—simply place it back on once the Peep has deflated. Enjoy immediately.

MOTHER'S DAY
Battenberg Cake

Need a cake to impress Mom (or mom-in-law)? Battenberg Cake is just the cake for the occasion. With its pink-and-white checkerboard pattern, it has a pinkies-out, fancy appearance that appears quite difficult to make—but truthfully, it's very straightforward. Your mom need never know how easy it was. She'll be so proud of you!

12 SERVINGS

1 cup (2 sticks) butter, softened

¾ cup sugar

1 teaspoon vanilla extract

2 large eggs

1½ cups all-purpose flour

2 teaspoons baking powder

¼ cup milk

Red food coloring

2 tablespoons amaretto (optional)

¼ cup apricot jam or your choice of preserves

11 ounces (1 can) almond paste

Preheat the oven to 350 degrees F.

Line a shallow 8- or 9-inch square cake pan with parchment paper. Construct a divider made of aluminum foil: I did this by taking a large, 14-inch expanse of foil and forming it by hand into a thick wedge the same length as the pan. It doesn't have to be prettily formed, as you will be trimming the edges of the cake it will be dividing, anyway.

In a stand mixer fitted with the paddle attachment, cream the butter, sugar, and vanilla until light and fluffy. Add the eggs one at a time, beating well after each addition, pausing occasionally to scrape down the sides of the bowl.

Sift the flour and baking powder together. Add to the egg mixture and mix just to combine. Add about 2 tablespoons of the milk and check the consistency (it should be soft, kind of like a drop-cookie dough). Add more milk as needed; you may not use the full ¼ cup. If using, stir in the amaretto until incorporated.

Divide the batter in two. Leave half of it plain; add red food coloring to the other half and mix it until you have a pink color a few shades more vibrant than you want the final product to be, since the color will fade slightly during baking. Pour each of the batters into separate sides of the prepared pan and spread them to fill the pan.

Bake for 30 to 35 minutes, or until the cakes are very lightly browned on the edges and have a dull finish on the top. Remove from the oven and let cool for about 15 minutes; turn out onto a wire rack and let cool fully.

Trim the edges of the cakes so that both pieces are the same size. Then cut each half lengthwise in two, so that you have four equal-size strips of cake.

Gently heat the apricot jam in a small pan or microwave-safe bowl until it liquefies. Spread a thin layer on the top of one of the strips of white cake, and use it to adhere one of the pink strips of cake on top. Repeat with the two remaining strips of cake, using the pink as the bottom layer, so that you have two cake "towers," one pink atop white, and the other white atop pink. Spread a thin layer of jam on the side of one of the stacks, and use it to stick both of them together. Voila, you now have a checkerboard pattern!

Wrap the cake in wax paper and let chill in the refrigerator for about half an hour—this will make it easier to handle in the following steps.

Near the end of the chilling period, on a clean surface, roll out the almond paste so that it is the length of the cake and wide enough to cover both sides (think of it like wrapping a gift—when in doubt, err on the larger side, as you can always trim away excess).

Remove the cake from the refrigerator and remove the wax paper. Brush the top with a thin coating of the preserves.

Invert the cake onto the rolled almond paste, then brush any uncovered surfaces with jam. This will help the almond paste stick.

Press the almond paste neatly around the cake, and turn it onto a serving tray. Let chill for 1 hour and serve in thick slices cut with a serrated knife.

Sweet and Salty Brownies

Two things I've learned about dudes who are dads: one, they always say they prefer salty snacks to sweets. Two, they always love brownies. So why not whip up a batch of brownies full of gooey caramel and then "man them up" with salty peanuts and pretzels? When these flavors all come together, you'll have an assault of awesome on the taste buds that will keep dad fat and happy.

CAKESPY NOTE: *If you have a favorite brownie recipe, feel free to use that and simply add in the last three ingredients for a sweet and salty upgrade.*

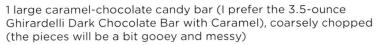

18 TO 24 BROWNIES

1¼ cups unsweetened cocoa powder

1¼ cups all-purpose flour

½ teaspoon salt

1½ cups (3 sticks) unsalted butter, melted

3 cups sugar

5 large eggs

2 teaspoons vanilla extract

½ cup chopped roasted, salted peanuts

1 large caramel-chocolate candy bar (I prefer the 3.5-ounce Ghirardelli Dark Chocolate Bar with Caramel), coarsely chopped (the pieces will be a bit gooey and messy)

1 snack-size bag (about 1 ounce) of pretzels or potato chips crushed into small pieces

3 cups Chocolate Fudge Buttercream Frosting (page 65) (optional)

Preheat the oven to 350 degrees F. Grease a 9-inch square baking pan, then line it with foil or parchment paper for easy removal and cutting later.

In a medium mixing bowl, combine the cocoa powder, flour, and salt; sift together and set aside.

To the bowl of a stand mixer fitted with the paddle attachment, add the melted butter and sugar; starting on a slow speed, beat them together until they form a cohesive, slightly gritty mixture.

Beat in the eggs one at a time, pausing to scrape down the sides of the bowl after each addition. Continue beating on medium speed until the mixture reaches a creamy consistency and is light yellow in color. Beat in the vanilla. Add the dry mixture, bit by bit, beating on low speed and continuing to scrape down the sides of the bowl until well blended. Using a large spoon or a rubber spatula, gently stir in the peanuts, chopped candy bar, and pretzels or chips.

Spread the batter evenly into the prepared pan.

Bake for 40 to 45 minutes, or until the brownies just begin to pull away from the edges of the pan. Let the brownies cool completely before frosting.

4TH OF JULY
Pop Rocks Cookies

Anyone can make red, white, and blue treats for the 4th of July. But to really American 'em up for the holiday, clearly you need to add explosive devices. Just like a summer blockbuster movie, these cookies are chock full of explosions: they're made and garnished with Pop Rocks. This not only makes them crackle like fireworks but also pays homage to that other all-consuming American obsession: truly trashy candy (I say this in the most loving way possible).

24 COOKIES, OR 12 COOKIE SANDWICHES

For the cookies:

½ cup (1 stick) butter, softened

⅔ cup sugar

¼ cup buttermilk

1 tablespoon vanilla extract

2 cups all-purpose flour, sifted

½ teaspoon baking soda

¼ teaspoon salt

5 drops red food coloring, plus more as needed

5 drops blue food coloring, plus more as needed

Six 0.24-ounce packages blue and red Pop Rocks candy (three packs for the cookies, three for garnish)

Sprinkles in red, white, and blue, to garnish

For the filling:

One 8-ounce package of cream cheese, softened (do not substitute low-fat)

½ cup butter, softened

2 teaspoons vanilla extract

¼ teaspoon salt

4 to 6 cups confectioners' sugar (depending on desired consistency)

Preheat the oven to 350 degrees F. Line two baking sheets with parchment paper.

In the bowl of a stand mixer fitted with the paddle attachment, beat the butter and sugar until smooth. Add the buttermilk and vanilla, beating until well combined, pausing occasionally to scrape down the sides of the bowl. The mixture may look a bit curdled; that's OK. Whisk together the flour, baking soda, and salt, then add them to the wet ingredients in several stages; beat until the mixture forms a cohesive dough.

Divide the dough into three parts, mixing one part with red food coloring and one part with blue; leave one part plain. At this point, you'll want to break into those Pop Rocks. Put the contents of one packet of red (strawberry) and one packet of blue (raspberry) into the corresponding balls of dough. Use whichever color you'd like in the white dough.

Using a 1-ounce cookie scoop (equal to 2 tablespoons of dough), spoon the dough onto the prepared baking sheets, leaving about 2 inches between the dough mounds.

Bake the cookies for 12 to 14 minutes, or until they are lightly brown on the edges. Allow them to cool for about 10 minutes, then transfer them to a wire rack to cool. The pop rocks may have caused some pockmarks in the cookies, but don't worry—they'll still taste good!

In a small bowl, mix your remaining packs of Pop Rocks with some red, white, and blue sprinkles. Using your fingers, give this mixture a quick stir to distribute the various colors of sprinkles and candy. Set to the side.

Prepare the frosting while the cookies cool. In a large mixing bowl, combine the cream cheese, butter, vanilla, and salt. Beat until the mixture has a very smooth consistency; pause to scrape the bowl as needed. Add the confectioners' sugar cup by cup, mixing after each addition, until it is smooth and spreadable.

Top each cookie with a generous dollop of frosting, or put a dollop between two cookies for a sandwich. If you've frosted the top of the cookie, apply some of the sprinkle mixture to the top (or dip it upside-down into the bowl if the frosting is thick enough); if you've made sandwiches, dip the edges in the bowl so that they pick up the sprinkle mixture. Serve immediately, since the Pop Rocks will lose their fizzle after a few hours.

LABOR DAY
Cakes Grilled in Orange Shells

In my opinion, there's a serious problem with Labor Day, our most grill-friendly holiday: a severe lack of cake. And so, in an effort to unearth cake recipes that might lend themselves to outdoor preparation, I consulted the most knowledgeable experts I could think of: the Boy Scouts. According to a vintage Boy Scouts camping recipe pamphlet I found at a local thrift store, these crafty boys have a sweet campfire trick up their sleeves: they bake their cakes over the fire in hollowed-out oranges. Strange as it may sound, it actually works. Beautifully.

12 TO 15 SERVINGS

12 large oranges, or 15 small oranges (types with a very thick rind work best)

1 batch of your favorite cake batter, homemade or from a mix

3 to 4 cups of your favorite frosting, such as Chocolate Fudge Buttercream (page 65)

Slice the top third off of each orange; set the top pieces to the side (you'll use them later, for garnish). Using a large spoon or a melon baller, scoop the fruit out of the oranges so that you have empty shells.

Prepare the cake batter according to the recipe, then fill each orange shell three-quarters full of cake batter.

Nestle each orange in a square of foil; place directly on a hot grill or on hot coals by a campfire for about 20 minutes, shifting them often to ensure even baking. Test each one for doneness by inserting a skewer into the middle of the cake; when it comes out clean, the cake is done. (Not grilling? Go ahead and bake the cakes in the oven. Still use the foil, as it will keep the orange shells from toppling over. Bake the cakes according to the time and temperature listed in your recipe; test with a skewer.)

At this point you have two options: you can let the cakes cool and then frost them liberally, then place the slices from the top portion of the orange jauntily on top as a garnish. Or, you can eat the warm unfrosted cake directly from the orange. Your choice.

Homemade Candy Corn

Ever wonder how candy corn is made? Well, to give you the short answer, with lots of heavy equipment, over a four- to five-day period. But don't let that process daunt you, because it is possible to make your own microbatches of the classic Halloween candy at home. This surprisingly simple recipe yields large, plump candy kernels infused with a sweet vanilla flavor. I find that using salted butter adds a nice, rich finish. Conclusion? These homespun tricolor treats are definitely worth the time and effort. Once you've tasted them, you may never buy candy corn by the bag again.

60 TO 80 PIECES CANDY CORN

2½ cups confectioners' sugar, sifted

⅓ cup powdered milk

1 cup granulated sugar

⅔ cup light corn syrup

⅓ cup salted butter

1 teaspoon vanilla extract

About 5 to 6 drops each red and yellow food coloring

In a medium bowl, whisk the confectioners' sugar with the powdered milk.

In a medium saucepan, combine the granulated sugar, corn syrup, and butter. Bring to a boil over high heat, stirring constantly. Once the mixture reaches the boiling point, reduce the heat to medium and continue cooking for about 5 minutes, stirring occasionally. The mixture will have reduced quite a bit and become rather thick. Stir in the vanilla and remove from the heat.

Add the confectioners' sugar mixture to the wet ingredients; stir well until the ingredients are thoroughly incorporated. The mixture will form a thick, smooth dough. Let the dough cool until it is firm enough to handle. You may leave it in the saucepan or transfer it to a bowl sprinkled with confectioners' sugar for quicker cooling.

Divide the dough into three equal parts and place each one into a separate bowl. Add 2 to 3 drops of yellow food coloring to one dish, one drop of red and two drops of yellow to another dish, and leave the remaining dish uncolored. Knead the doughs to which you have added food coloring until the color is even (use gloves to avoid staining your hands). If the dough is very soft or sticky, you may want to chill it for about 5 minutes in the refrigerator before proceeding with the next steps.

Place each piece of dough on top of a sheet of waxed paper or parchment paper, and then use your hands to roll each color of dough into a long, slender rope about ¼ to ½ inch in diameter (the larger the diameter, the easier they will be to handle, although if you want a realistically sized end result, make your rolls more slender).

Lay the three ropes of dough side by side, touching each other: white, orange, and yellow. To ensure that they stick together, lay a piece of waxed or parchment paper on top and press very gently with a rolling pin. You just want to help them adhere to one another, not to flatten them.

Using a very sharp knife, cut the dough into triangles. Keep a damp cloth nearby so that you can wipe off the knife if a candy residue begins to build up. Let the finished kernels set for an hour or two in the open air until they are quite dry and firm (do not stack them on top of one another or they will stick together!). Store in a single layer in a cool, dry place.

Leftover Cranberry Sauce Bar Cookies

The year's biggest eating weekend is over (sigh). But there's definitely some sweet eating to be had from what few leftovers we haven't yet eaten, as proven by these cranberry nut squares. This is a revamped version of a pecan bar but is composed instead with leftover cranberry sauce and the mixed nuts that play a supporting role in so many Thanksgiving recipes. The resulting jewel-toned bars are surprisingly addictive: sweet, salty, tart, tangy, and buttery all at once.

18 TO 24 SERVINGS

For the crust:
¾ cup (1½ sticks) unsalted butter, softened

⅓ cup sugar

1½ cups all-purpose flour

¼ teaspoon salt

For the topping:
1 cup light corn syrup

¾ cup packed brown sugar

2 tablespoons unsalted butter

1 teaspoon vanilla extract

2 large eggs, beaten

1¼ cups cranberry sauce, or 1 cup dried cranberries

1½ cups toasted nuts of your choice (I prefer salted mixed nuts)

Preheat the oven to 375 degrees F. Grease a 9-by-13-inch pan.

In a stand mixer fitted with the paddle attachment, beat the butter with the sugar at medium speed until light and fluffy, about 2 minutes, scraping the bowl as needed. Add the flour and salt and mix on low speed until a soft dough forms. Press the dough evenly into the bottom of the prepared pan, forming the edges about ½ inch up the sides of the pan. Bake in the center of the oven for 12 to 15 minutes, until the crust is golden and set. Let cool on a wire rack.

Reduce the oven temperature to 325 degrees F.

Meanwhile, prepare the filling. In a medium saucepan, combine the corn syrup, brown sugar, butter, and vanilla over medium heat until everything has melted and formed a thick syrup. Continue stirring over medium heat until it bubbles around the edges but has not quite reached a boil. Remove the mixture from the heat and let it cool for about 10 minutes, stirring occasionally to speed the cooling process. Then, whisk in the beaten eggs, stirring vigorously. Set aside.

Spread the cranberry sauce evenly on top of the baked and cooled crust. If you are using dried cranberries, scatter them evenly. Scatter the nuts on top of the cranberry layer.

Pour the liquid mixture over everything. It is a thick mixture—try to pour it so that you get even coverage over the other toppings. If needed, use a spatula to distribute it, but be gentle so that you do not tear up the bottom crust layer.

Bake for 45 to 50 minutes, or until the filling is lightly bubbling on the sides and looks firm in the middle. Let cool thoroughly before cutting—the filling will continue to firm up as the bars cool.

HANUKKAH
Marshmallow Dreidels

One year, I hosted a cookie swap and someone brought chocolate-covered dreidels. It was a bit perplexing, as the person who brought them didn't celebrate Hanukkah—but when pressed, he had a valid reason for choosing them: "I thought they were cute!" They certainly were, and they disappeared quicker than you can spin a dreidel.

12 DREIDELS

1¼ cups chocolate chips, dark or milk chocolate, or 1¼ cups blue-toned candy melts, such as Merckens

12 jumbo marshmallows

12 to 16 thin, 3- to 4-inch-long pretzel sticks (the kind that come in those mini snack packs)

12 chocolate "kisses" or nonpareils

One tube white decorating icing

Line a baking sheet with wax paper or parchment paper.

In a double boiler or microwave-safe bowl, melt the chocolate chips or candy melts, stirring frequently to prevent scorching. Remove from the heat.

Spear each marshmallow with a pretzel stick, making sure that it goes three-fourths of the way through. Dip the bottom of a chocolate kiss into the melted chocolate and adhere it to the other end of the marshmallow. Place it on its side on the waxed paper to set. Repeat with the remaining marshmallows. Put them in the refrigerator for about 30 minutes to ensure that the components have adhered to one another.

Gently reheat the chocolate so that it is soft and melty again. Using the pretzel stick as a handle, dip one of your treats into the chocolate so that it is coated up to the top of the marshmallow. Return it to the baking sheet and repeat

with the remaining dreidels. This will leave one side of the chocolate coating slightly flattened, but that's OK—it will make them stay put on the serving dish.

Using the white decorating icing, add Hebrew letters to the sides of the dreidels. I find that for newbies, the hay symbol, which vaguely resembles the pi sign, is the easiest to draw. Or, if you're not too handy with Hebrew, Stars of David or snowflakes are nice, if not technically dreidel-accurate.

Let the dreidels set for about 30 minutes before serving.

CHRISTMAS
Ginger-Bread Pudding

Once Christmas is over, what to do with the leftovers? Resist the urge to do anything rash like start New Year's resolutions early. Instead, make the best of the rest of the year by combining your leftover eggnog, gingerbread, and some butter and eggs to form a delicious Ginger-Bread Pudding. It's easy as can be to make and very forgiving with substitutions. Want to make it with cinnamon rolls or doughnuts instead of ginger-bread? Go for it!

CAKESPY NOTE: *If you're using a non-gingerbread carbohydrate for your bread pudding, you can add spices such as cinnamon, ginger, and nutmeg to taste.*

8 SERVINGS

3 tablespoons cold butter, in one chunk, plus extra for buttering dish

3 cups cubed leftover soft gingerbread or other quick bread or pound cake or other bread-like product

2 large eggs

2 cups eggnog or heavy cream

1 teaspoon vanilla extract

½ teaspoon salt

Butter an 8-inch square baking dish or a 9-inch pie plate.

Cube your carbohydrate of choice. Spread evenly in the buttered baking dish.

In a small bowl, whisk the eggs. Add the eggnog, vanilla, and salt, then whisk to combine. Gently pour this mixture over the cubed gingerbread. Let this soak while you preheat the oven to 350 degrees F.

Using a vegetable peeler, shave the cold butter directly onto the top of your casserole. (No, this is not strictly necessary, but—so delicious.) Bake for 30 to 40 minutes, or until the filling is just barely set in the middle and the top is browned.

... onward into the sweetness!

Index

About the Author

photo by Mike Hipple

JESSIE OLESON is a triple threat: writer/illustrator/gallery owner. After attending Pratt Institute in Brooklyn and working at two stationery companies, she branched off to start her own business. Going under the alter-ego of CakeSpy, she has a blog where she writes about dessert, and a retail gallery where she mostly sells drawings of dessert. In addition to a weekly column on foodie website SeriousEats.com, she has also done illustration work for various companies including Microsoft, iPop, All-Mighty, Taylored Expressions, and Taste of Home. She lives in Seattle with her husband, Danny; two pugs, Olive and Porkchop; and a fridge that is always very well stocked with butter.